1. 25 November 1940 and Brigadier-General Walthall inspects Home Guard units at Chaddesden.

2. A new look for Derby Corporation buses came in January 1940 when it was decided that women could be employed as conductressees as an answer to staff shortages.

DERBY
AT
WAR

Second Edition

3. Tank Fund Rag Day, 27 September 1941.

Clive Hardy
Russ Brown

First published 1979
This edition published 1989 by
Quoin Publishing Limited
The Barn
36A North Road, Kirkburton, Huddersfield,
West Yorkshire HD8 0RH

Printed in the UK by
Netherwood Dalton & Company Limited
Bradley Mills
Huddersfield

ISBN 1 85563 002 8

4A. HRH The Duke of Kent chats with workers during his visit to the Bliss Shell Factory,
City Road 5 March 1941. *Courtesy* E. W. Bliss.

Contents

Introduction

The purpose of this, the second edition of *Derby at War* , is to present a photographic record of life in and around our city during the Second World War, a conflict that directly affected the lives of every man, woman and child. It is not meant to be a definitive work in any way, as space does not permit it to be, but an attempt has been made to recapture the atmosphere of fifty years ago, when this country fought for its very survival against Nazi aggression, and, for a whole year of war fought alone.

As well as concentrating on everyday life in Derby, which was forced to adapt to the stringent demands of war with the rationing of food, fuel and clothing and the rigorous attention being paid to the vital area of Air Raid Precautions, this book has also tried to capture something of the experiences of the men and women of Derby enlisted in the services, who may have spent the whole war away from their families.

Many new photographs have been included in this new edition and the text has all but been rewritten. New subjects covered include photographs of ENSA and other Concert Parties; sections on the Home Guard; Land Workers and agriculture; the balloon barrage; the Sherwood Foresters Regiment; the Derbyshire Yeomanry; the ATS; Indian troops stationed in the locality; the ATC; and postwar pictures of refugee Dutch children in Derby.

The photographs and information have been drawn from a wide range of sources and we hope that we have duly acknowledged everyone who contributed their time and who shared their memories with us, in the acknowledgements at the back of the book. Please forgive any omissions.

June 1989

Clive Hardy
Russ Brown

4B. The Arboretum bandstand, bombed January 1941.

The Road to War

In May 1937 following Stanley Baldwin's resignation, Neville Chamberlain was appointed Prime Minister. Chamberlain was nearly seventy years old, had a lean hawkish look about him, and always dressed in forbidding dark clothes and wing collars.

As Prime Minister, he proved to be obstinate, impatient of criticism and secretive. He could be a natural dictator and ruled his Cabinet with a rod of iron that has only been matched by that of Margaret Thatcher. Chamberlain was also blessed with an undemocratic arrogance to the point of ignoring parliament and evading debate, and, on top of all this he distrusted officials at the Foreign Office and would not hesitate in circumventing them in order to get his own way and pursue his own brand of personal diplomacy. In matters of foreign policy he had no love for the Soviet Union whatsoever and his dealings with France, though inescapable, proved to be far from cordial. Above all else, his hatred of war was without doubt both passionate and sincere. He followed what he himself called a "general scheme of appeasement" in the belief that it would solve Europe's problems and save us from ever again experiencing the senseless slaughter of the Great War.

The League of Nations had been established after the Great War in an attempt to promote international peace through collective security. However, during the inter-war years the League ideal failed. The United States withdrew into isolationism, ignoring European affairs though all the Allies were heavily in debt to her. In the Far East Imperial Japan embarked on economic, political and military expansionism, invading China's northern province of Manchuria in September 1931 with impunity. When the Italian dictator Benito Mussolini took the first steps in carving out a new Roman Empire in North Africa by invading and annexing Abyssinia, the League dithered for ten months before voting to impose only the most limited of sanctions upon the aggressor. It would also fail to act decisively in the Spanish Civil War, and Germany's acquisition of Austria and Czechoslovakia.

Adolf Hitler came to power in Germany in January 1933 when the Nazis polled 37.3 per cent of the popular vote in the general election giving them 230 seats in the Reichstag and making them the largest single party in parliament. For fifteen years, the Weimar Republic had experienced economic and political chaos but Hitler was determined to put an end to such carryings on by restoring Germany to her pre-1914 position as the leading European power.

Hitler was without doubt a political opportunist but he was also a charismatic figure who from 1934 onwards pushed rearmament and reinflation to the very limit. It was not an easy task as Germany lacked essential raw materials, apart from coal, and had to rely on imports which were often subjected to sporadic delivery due to the lack of foreign exchange with which to pay for them. By 1937 the German economy was on a knife's edge, there was a serious shortage of steel and many factories were running at less than 80 per cent capacity. As late as January 1939, Hitler had little alternative but to announce reductions in the allocation of raw materials for the armaments industry amounting to steel, 30 per cent; copper, 20 per cent; concrete, 45 per cent; rubber, 14 per cent; and aluminium 47 per cent.

Hitler believed that the Reich's economic problems could be solved by the annexation of territory to the east and the retaking of land taken from her by the Treaty of Versailles. He believed that the time was right to pursue this course of action because of the inability of the League of Nations to act; the isolationist policies of the United States; Britain and France's diplomatic ineptness due to their policy of "non-intervention"; and the Soviet Union's inability to act militarily because of Stalin's purges of the Communist Party and the armed forces.

On 9 March 1935, Germany admitted that she possessed an air force (*Luftwaffe*) which had grown in less than two years to an establishment of 900 flying officers and 17,000 men, though unbeknown to the outside world, the indigenous aircraft industry still lacked the capacity for large-scale military production. One week later, Germany introduced conscription to raise the strength of the army by 450,000 men from the Treaty of Versailles ceiling of 100,000 regulars.

In 1936, in contravention of the Treaty of Versailles, Hitler ordered troops into the demilitarized Rhineland. Britain and France, who could have successfully intervened, did nothing. Over the following two years, Britain and France's unwillingness to stand up to Germany either militarily or diplomatically would mislead Hitler. and the High Command and contribute to the eventual decision to attack Poland.

The German incorporation of Austria into the Reich in March 1936 went totally unchallenged by the Allies despite a joint declaration on Austrian independence in February 1934 by Great Britain, France and Italy. In 1938, Britain and France's handling of the Czech Crisis was disgraceful. Neither Chamberlain nor the French President, Daladier, knew how to handle Hitler.

In February 1938, Hitler gave a speech in which he promised protection for all Germans living outside the Reich. The speech was seized upon by Sudeten Nazis in Czechoslovakia to intensify their demands for self-determination. In the ensuing crisis, Britain determined that she would not get involved militarily and France, who was bound by treaty to aid Czechoslovakia in the event of war, reneged on her obligations. The French panicked at the thought of being left to fight a European war on their own and Daladier begged Chamberlain to do something, anything, that would get France off the hook.

With Germany threatening war, the French abdicated all initiatives to Britain. Chamberlain flew to Berchtesgaden to see Hitler.

Behind the scenes, however, the German armed forces were in no fit state to get involved in a shooting war. The army was still expanding and was seriously short of officers and NCO's. Many units were untrained and there was only six weeks supply of ammunition. The *Luftwaffe* was in the middle of a transition period caused by new types of aircraft introduced from 1936 onwards. The whole of the *Luftwaffe* was only 57 per cent operational and reserves of some aircraft lubricants and spares stood at only six per cent of the mobilization requirement.

Germany's trump card was her propaganda machine. Throughout the summer, a superbly conducted campaign led Europe to believe that Germany's fighting capability was far greater than it actually was. Visiting dignitaries were taken from one airfield to another to witness the might of the *Luftwaffe*. What the dignitaries weren't privy to was the fact that some squadrons of modern aircraft were leap-frogging from one airfield to another ahead of them thus giving the impression that the *Luftwaffe's* operational strength was greater that it actually was. The Czechs were abandoned to their fate.

The decision to attack Poland was partially based on the fact that Hitler had convinced himself that despite some sabre rattling, Great Britain would do little to stop him, especially if the campaign were to last only several weeks. Another reason was that Germany would regain control of the whole of Upper Silesia, second only to the Ruhr in industrial importance and immensely rich in coal, iron and zinc. The area had been divided between Poland and Germany after the war but the Polish territory contained 53 out of 67 coalmines; 21 out of 37 blast furnaces; 9 out of 14 rolling mills; and 70 per cent of the entire zinc output.

On 22 August 1939, Hitler met with his senior military advisers and announced that the time had come to settle accounts with Poland. One of the factors for war was economic "our economic situation is such that we can only hold out for a few more years." Others were military. "As neither France nor Britain can achieve any decisive successes in the West, and as Germany, as a result of the agreement with Russia, will have all her forces free in the East after the defeat of Poland, and as air superiority is undoubtedly on our side, I do not shrink from solving the Eastern question even at the risk of complication in the West."

6. February 1939. Some of the twenty-nine Czech refugees who were billeted at Ilam Hall await transport from Derby LMS Station.

7. British Government policy towards Czechoslovakia was both ill-informed and unsympathetic. France, which was bound by treaty to aid Czechoslovakia in the event of war, feared that if it came to a fight Britain might remain neutral. Outwardly the Anglo-French conversations were shown as the working-out of a joint policy towards Germany's demands. Behind the scenes, however, both governments had decided to abandon the Czechs to their fate, but a public announcement of that fact would have been political suicide. The above photograph shows Czech refugees at the LMS Station. The Derby Committee for the Care of Czech Refugees had arranged for this group to go to Farley Hall.

On Saturday 2 September, 2,200 school children were evacuated from Kedleston Road, Central Nursery (Nuns Street), St Mary's in Orchard Street, Gerard Street, First Estate and Ashbourne Roads schools. Evacuation plans for secondary schools were announced, though the evacuation of expectant mothers and the disabled was postponed.

From Derby, 1,000 evacuees were sent to the Chesterfield/Clay Cross area, 1,000 to North Wingfield, 300 to New Tupton and Pilsley, 250 to Stonebrook, 200 to Shirland and 150 to Morton.

The following day 2,100 more children went from Traffic Street, St Andrews, Clarence Road, St James Road Infants, Pear Tree and Reginald Street schools. Secondary schools commenced evacuation at 7.50am with Homelands followed by the Central School for Boys, Parkfield Cedars, and Bemrose.

8/9. On Saturday, 2 September 1939, Derby began to evacuate its children. *Below:* Evacuees prepare to leave from Reginald Street School, 3 September 1939

10. Evacuated children arriving at Ripley Station.

11. It's smile for the camera (well nearly all smiles) from this group of evacuees.

12. Team and supporters line up. This is one of the teams playing in a competition held by evacuees at Ripley.

13. Derby evacuees at Ockbrook, November 1939.

14. Some boys from Derby School at their 'war home' at Overton Hall. Can you spot TV celebrity Ted Moult?

4th SEPTEMBER, 1939

GOLD MUST BE SOLD TO THE TREASURY

If you have any gold coins you must take it to the bank and sell it to the Treasury. Luxury imports, including motor-cars, clothing and perfumery, are banned.

These regulations were issued last night.

Residents in Britain must offer foreign securities and bullion, as well as gold coin, to their bankers.

Foreign exchange to be offered for sale includes currencies named by the Treasury from time to time. Those already named include:—

U.S. dollars, Guilders, Canadian dollars, Argentine pesos, Belgas, Swedish crowns, Swiss francs, Norwegian crowns and French francs.

Persons may apply through their bankers for permission to retain gold and foreign exchange required to meet contracts, made before the coming into force of these regulations, which provide for payments in gold or foreign exchange, for meeting the reasonable requirements of trade or business, or for reasonable travelling or other personal expenses.

Prices to be paid for gold and foreign exchange offered for sale are to be determined by the Treasury, and may be ascertained by inquiry at any bank.

The public should continue to transact business in foreign exchange and gold through the agency of their bankers.

Applications for exchange must be made on the appropriate form, and satisfactory evidence in regard to the transaction proposed must be produced in all cases.

Export of banknotes, gold, securities or foreign currency is prohibited except with permission.

Traders Must Insure

The order issued by the Board of Trade bans the imports, except under licence, of luxuries and goods of which there are sufficient home supplies.

This will conserve exchange for the additional purchases of other products required in war time.

The main categories of goods covered by the order are pottery and glass, cutlery, clocks and watches, textile goods and apparel (including footwear), certain chemicals and paints, soap, office machinery (including typewriters), motor-cars, musical instruments, perfumery and toilet requisites, toys and games and luxury foodstuffs.

Traders in Britain who sell goods liable to King's enemy risks must insure them under the War Risks Insurance Act.

This is part of a scheme which the Board of Trade has put into operation.

Liability of the Board as insurers will be determined by a policy of insurance issued in a form prescribed in the schedule of the War Risks (Commodity Insurance) (No. 1) Order.

Insurance is compulsory except where the value of a person's insurable goods does not exceed £1,000.

BILLETS BY ORDER, IF—

A FEW householders who have so far been unwilling to receive evacuees are asked not to force the Government to exercise compulsion.

Making this appeal yesterday, Sir Warren Fisher, the North-West Regional Commissioner, pointed out:

"It is not possible at present to say how long the billets will last.

"But all must be prepared for danger and hardship, and will be lucky if it takes no worse a form than receiving strangers into one's house.

"No war can be won under modern conditions unless the essential work of the towns can be continued in spite of air raids. This will be easier if the townspeople in dangerous areas can be relieved of anxiety for their young children.

"It is also of vital importance to preserve the lives of children, who will be the citizens of the next generation, so that householders in safer districts must take them in.

"Parliament has given powers to billet them compulsorily in the reception areas, and the Government is determined to use those powers if necessary."

HITLER BLAMES BRITAIN

HITLER, in messages to his Army of the West and to the German people yesterday, blamed Britain for the war.

He claimed that the Poles had "attacked" Germany, and that he was fighting to "establish peace." He added that he was on the way to the Eastern Front.

To his troops on the Western Front he said (according to the German News Agency, quoted by Reuter):—

"The British Government, driven on by those warmongers whom we knew in the last war, has resolved to let fall its mask and to proclaim war on a threadbare pretext.

"For months it (the British Government) has supported the Polish attacks against the lives and security of fellow-Germans and the rape of the Free City of Danzig," continued Hitler.

"In a Few Months"

"Now that Poland, with the consciousness of this protection, has undertaken acts of aggression against Reich territory, I have determined to blow up this ring which has been laid round Germany.

"Sections of the German Army in the East have now, for two days, in response to Polish attacks, been fighting for the establishment of a peace which shall assure life and freedom to the German people.

"If you do your duty, the battle in the East will have reached its successful conclusion in a few months, and then the power of the whole Nazi State stands behind you.

"As an old soldier of the world war, and as your supreme commander, I am going, with confidence in you, to the Army on the East."

"Unity or—" Threat

To the German people Hitler said the English "encirclement" policy was resumed when the "peaceful" revision of the Versailles Treaty seemed to be succeeding.

To this he added: "The same lying inciters appeared as in 1914."

Claiming that "as long as the German people was united it has never been conquered," Hitler uttered this threat:—

"Whoever offends against this unity need expect nothing else than annihilation as an enemy of the nation."

DUKE TAKES UP NAVAL POST

The Admiralty announces that Rear-Admiral His Royal Highness the Duke of Kent has taken up his war appointment.

Immediately after Mr. Chamberlain's dramatic broadcast to the nation, the Government yesterday announced a number of precautionary measures to prevent people crowding together and so increasing the casualty risks from air raids.

Instructions were given for the closing of all places of entertainment until further notice. In the light of experience it may be possible to open cinemas and theatres in some areas later. Included in the closure orders are indoor and outdoor sports gatherings where large numbers of people might be expected to congregate.

The following advice is given:—

Keep off the streets as much as possible; to expose yourself unnecessarily adds to your danger.

Carry your gas mask with you always.

Make sure every member of your household have on them their names and addresses clearly written. Do this on an envelope or luggage label and not on an odd piece of paper which may be lost.

Sew a label on children's clothing so that they cannot pull it off.

People are requested not to crowd together unnecessarily in any circumstances.

Churches and other places of public worship will not be closed.

All day schools in evacuation and neutral areas in England, Wales and Scotland are to be closed for lessons for at least a week from yesterday.

In the reception areas schools will be opened as soon as evacuation is complete.

BANKS ARE SHUT TO-DAY

TO-DAY has been declared a limited Bank Holiday, affecting only banks. The arrangement applies to the Post Office Savings Bank and other savings banks.

This day will be used by the banks to complete their measures for adapting themselves to the emergency, and to-morrow morning the banks will be open for business.

The Treasury, in conjunction with the Bank of England, have taken all the steps needed to ensure that the banks (including the Post Office Savings Bank and other savings banks) will be amply supplied with currency.

Postal orders will be legal tender for the present, and Scottish and Northern Ireland banknotes will be legal tender in Scotland and Northern Ireland respectively.

AIR MAIL CURTAILED

Empire air mail services are from to-day restricted to two services weekly in each direction between the United Kingdom and Sydney and one weekly in each direction between the United Kingdom and Durban and between the United Kingdom and Kisumu.

Corresponding modifications will be made in the overseas connecting services operated by Imperial Airways.

Present arrangements under which first-class mail to certain countries is forwarded by Empire Air Mail services without surcharge will be suspended, and a surcharge will be imposed on all mail from the United Kingdom carried by air on the Empire routes.

Day-old Babies Leave

Three babies born only the previous day were among three trainloads of evacuees from London yesterday.

Accompanied by their mothers, they were driven in an ambulance from the station to a nursing home which has been taken over as a maternity home.

Cinemas, Theatres Close to Cut Risks

PETROL IS RATIONED

PETROL rationing will be introduced, as from September 16.

This was announced last night by the Secretary for Mines. Information as to how the public can secure their ration books will be announced to-day.

There are very substantial stocks of petrol in the country, but in the national interests the best use must be made of these supplies.

Petrol distributors have arranged to pool all their resources and, after the individual brands still in stock at garages and service stations have been sold by them at prices now ruling, one grade only of motor spirit will be supplied to the public.

This spirit will be called "Pool" motor spirit, and will be on sale, ex-pump, in England and Wales at 1s. 6d. a gallon.

Appeal to Owners

No change will be made in the price for the next fourteen days at least. From to-day no further supplies of individual brands will be made at garages and service stations.

For at least the same period of fourteen days there will be no change in yesterday's bulk prices to those commercial concerns who receive their supplies direct.

Owners and drivers of commercial vehicles are particularly asked to note that it will no longer be possible to allow commercial vehicles to call at petrol companies' depots for supplies.

The Government appeal to all owners of motor vehicles to use them only for essential purposes.

U.S. REFUGEES LEAVE LONDON

BETWEEN two and three thousand American refugees left London last night. Many of them were destitute.

An American Embassy official said it might take ten days before sufficient ships to evacuate these people will have put in.

Mr. Joseph Kennedy, American Ambassador, has requested all American and other neutral steamship lines to provide all available ships, including freighters and tankers, for evacuation.

WARNINGS TO SHIPPING

The Board of Trade announces: "Shipping is hereby warned that all traffic proceeding through the Dover Straits must proceed through the Downs. Ships disregarding this warning do so at their own peril."

The Admiralty give notice that vessels entering the Firth of Forth must pass to the northward of Bass Rock. Vessels proceeding to the southward of Bass Rock will do so at their own peril.

The Home Front

On 27th September 1939, Sir John Simon introduced the Emergency War Budget, The first commodity to be rationed was petrol. An increase in whisky duty was expected to bring in £3,500,000 in a full year. The basic duty on tobacco was increased from 11s 6d to 13s 6d per pound, adding 1 ½d per ounce to the price in the shops. Sugar duty was also increased which led to high prices in the shops of tinned fruit, jam, marmalade, syrup, and sweetened milk.

On 28th December, the Press carried news that the rationing of meat would be introduced on 15th January 1940. W. S. Morrison, Minister of Food, announced that the intended ration was to be 6 oz. per head per day, though it was expected that this would be for prime cuts only and that cheaper cuts of beef, mutton, or pork would still be available for purchase up to the value of six ounces of prime cut. The rationing would not apply to tinned meats, fowl, rabbit and 'offal'.

The rationing of basic food stuffs was introduced in January 1940. The weekly allowance per person included 2 ozs tea (none for the under fives), 2 ozs of fats. Extra cheese was allowed to those workers who had no canteen facilities, and a special ration was available to vegetarians who undertook to surrender their meat coupons. Bacon and ham were rationed at 1s 11d per lb for Middle, 2s 1d per lb for ham/gammon, and at 1s 6d per lb for shoulder. Other cuts were priced at 1s 4d per lb for first quality Topside (second quality and imported cuts were 2d per lb cheaper), 1s 6d per lb for first quality mutton and 2s 2d per lb for prime rump steak; again, second quality and imported cuts were a few pence per pound cheaper.

The 1940 Budget, when it was announced, was to that date the largest sum ever raised in one years taxation in British history. Income tax was raised from 7s to 7s 6d in the pound and surtax was levied on those whose incomes exceeded £1,500 a year. Beer went up by 1d a pint, whisky by 1s 9d a bottle to 16s; tobacco duty was increased by 3d an ounce and matches by a ½d a box. Postal charges for inland letters went up by 1d to 2½d, and all inland telephone calls by 15 per cent. That same year the 'points' system of rationing was introduced for clothing and tinned meats. Tinned salmon, crab, oranges, pineapples, lemons and so on were not officially rationed because they were almost impossible to get hold of.

At the beginning of 1945 the weekly basic ration was 4 ozs bacon, 2 ozs tea, 8 ozs sugar, meat to the value of 1s 2d, 8 ozs of fats, 3 ozs of cheese and two pints of milk. In March the milk ration was increased by an extra half pint per person per week, but by May shortages led to reductions in bacon and lard rations. The clothing ration in 1945 was 48 coupons. A man's suit made of utility cloth took 24 coupons, and soldiers being discharged early on medical grounds could make a small fortune by selling their demob outfits. . .

MINISTRY OF FOOD

YOUR NEW RATION BOOK

HOW TO REGISTER WITH THE SHOPS

The new Ration Books are now being distributed. As soon as you receive your new Book you must fill in the particulars as explained below, and then take the Book to the shops for fresh Registration. It has been found possible to allow *immediate* Registration, and the sooner you register the better.

IF 50 PEOPLE DON'T TRAVEL

1 TANK CAN

*At this most important time
Needless travel is a "crime"*

BRITISH RAILWAYS
GWR — LMS — LNER — SR

UNITED TO WIN THE WAR

19/20. 12 September 1939. Anxious passengers study the emergency passenger timetables at Derby LMS Station. As the war progressed the Railway Executive Committee actively discouraged people from using trains unless their journey was essential to the war effort. In any case, all passenger trains were restricted to a maximum top speed of 60mph, which meant that the journey from London to Edinburgh took 8hrs 40min compared with 7hrs 20min before the war. By the summer of 1944 occasional excursions were again running – but not over vast distances. Typical destinations from Derby were Sutton Bonnington Agricultural College or the University of Nottingham. *Below:* February 1940. A special coal train on the LMS line at Breadsall with an urgent delivery caused by the coal shortage. The coal shortage was due both to a severe cold spell at the begining of the year and the drop in coal output due to large numbers of miners volunteering for the armed forces.

21. Ration books at the ready at the Food Office, Derby.

22/24. Despite the general unease facing Europe since the Czech crisis of 1938, little was done by the British Government to build up reserves of food, fuel and essential raw materials. As the Second World War loomed ever closer, both the Cabinet and the Admiralty considered that the main threat to our merchant ships would come from German surface raiders. The submarine threat, whilst not being overlooked, was pushed into the background, with too much faith being placed in ASDIC, the Royal Navy's anti-submarine detection equipment. Whilst ASDIC was a remarkable piece of equipment it was not as efficient as many people had been led to believe.

In September 1939, the German U-boat Arm comprised 56 submarines of which only 22 were ocean-going boats capable of operating in the Atlantic. When hostilities commenced both Britain and Germany had every available submarine already deployed on their respective war stations. In the first month of the war 40 merchant and fishing vessels were sunk by U-boats, nine were sunk by mines, and only one, the *Clement*, was sunk by a surface raider – a grand total of 189,000 tons. By the end of the year the U-boats had claimed 103 victims; 83 others had been sunk by mines, fifteen by surface raiders and ten by the *Luftwaffe* – a total of 746,000 tons.

The rationing of basic foodstuffs was introduced in January 1940, and the middle photograph on this page shows shoppers waiting for their supplies of meat at a stall in Derby Market Hall in February 1940. The photograph below was taken in May 1943 and shows the queue for ration books at the food offices in The Strand.

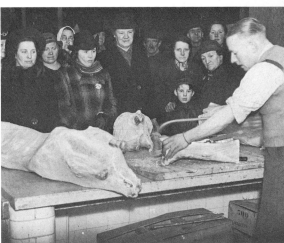

25-26. "If you see a queue . . . join it!" It wasn't uncommon to join a queue without knowing what particular goody was to be had at the other end, especially so after Sir Stafford Cripps had told the House of Commons in February 1942 that "personal extravagance must be eliminated altogether." The two photographs pre-date Sir Stafford's edict by ten months. *Above:* A queue for cakes and pastries outside Birds in St James's Street. *Below:* A similar scene outside the Co-op.

Single Persons

Earned Income £	Present Tax £ s. d.			New Tax Fo[r] 1940-41 £ s.	
125	—	—	—	15	
130		9	4	1	11
200	7	0	0	12	10
250	11	13	4	20	6
300	17	10	0	28	2
400	45	10	0	56	11
500	73	10	0	87	16
600	101	10	0	119	1
700	129	10	0	150	6
800	157	10	0	181	11
1000	213	10	0	244	1

Childless Married Couples

£	£	s.	d.	£	s.
225	—	—	—	3	5
250	2	6	8	7	3
300	7	0	0	15	0
400	17	10	0	30	12
500	45	10	0	61	11
600	73	10	0	92	16
700	101	10	0	124	1
800	129	10	0	155	6
1000	185	10	0	217	16
2000	500	10	0	561	11

Married Couples With One Child

£	£	s.	d.	£	s.
300	—	—	—	5	12
350	4	13	4	13	8
400	9	6	8	21	5
500	24	10	0	42	6
600	52	10	0	74	1
700	80	10	0	105	6
800	108	10	0	136	11
1000	164	10	0	199	1
2000	479	10	0	542	16

Married Couples With Two Children

£	£	s.	d.	£	
350	—	—	—	4	1
400	2	6	8	11	17
500	11	13	4	27	10
600	31	10	0	55	6
700	59	10	0	86	11
800	87	10	0	117	16
1000	143	10	0	180	6
2000	458	10	0	524	1

Married Couples With Three Children

£	£	s.	d.	£	s. d.
400	—	—	—	2	10
500	4	13	4	18	2
600	14	0	0	36	11
700	38	10	0	67	16
800	66	10	0	99	1
1000	122	10	0	161	11
2000	437	10	0	505	6

Only deductions in abov[e] tables are personal allowanc[e] and earned income relief fo[r] single persons, married and children allowances and earned income relief fo[r] others.

★

Surtax becomes payabl[e] from £1,500 instead o[f] £2,000, but the increase wil[l] not be demanded unti[l] January 1, 1942.

27. The effect on earnings of raising income tax from 7s to 7s6d in the pound, Budget Day 1940.

28. In the early days of rationing, cookery demonstrations were something of a regular event showing housewives how to make their food stocks go that little bit further.

PART 1 IN THE POTATO PLAN

Parsley Potato Cakes

Potatoes for Breakfast

three days a week

Potatoes taste grand for breakfast. Try them! Here's a good suggestion: Parsley Potato Cakes. Are you watching out for other recipes in this series?

PARSLEY POTATO CAKES

Boil an extra pound of potatoes the day before you want to make the cakes. Mash these while hot, with a little milk, and seasoning of salt and pepper to taste.

Next day, add a tablespoon of chopped parsley and shape the mixture into little cakes. Cover with browned breadcrumbs, and pan-fry in a little hot fat, or bake in the oven. The mixture should not be made wet.

The 4 other parts of the Plan:

2 Make your main dish a potato dish one day a week.

3 Refuse second helpings of other food. Have more potatoes instead.

4 Serve potatoes in other ways than " plain boiled."

5 Use potatoes in place of flour (part potatoes, part flour).

Bread costs ships . . .
Eat home-grown potatoes instead

31. The LMS Fuel Economy Coach visits the East Midlands. Visitors to the exhibition were urged to economise on gas, electricity, coal and hot water. "Only five inches of hot water in your bath . . . more hot water for the Nazis!"

5 lbs. OF COAL SAVED IN ONE DAY BY 40,000 HOMES WILL PROVIDE ENOUGH FUEL TO BUILD A CHURCHILL TANK

NOTE: 5 lbs. of coal are used in 2 hours by a gas fire or electric oven.

33. Save coal help build a tank. Every piece of salvageable metal was recycled including pots and pans which were turned into aircraft.

32. A party of scouts head for Robshaws with a barrow-load of waste paper. Everything possible was salvaged: old clothing, newspapers, metal and even food scraps, which ultimately ended up as pig feed.

COAL

Use Coal carefully
Be glad of any Coal
Don't worry about the kind
Your merchant will supply
    the best he can

Ask your supplier for FREE
booklets on how to save coal and coke
and watch these hints.

NEVER WASTE HOT WATER
NEVER USE SOOTY PANS
NEVER FORCE THE BOILER

ISSUED BY THE MINES DEPARTMENT

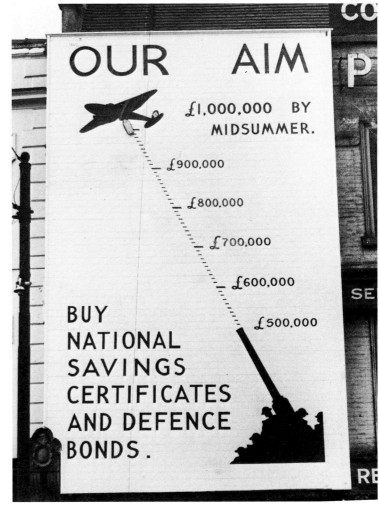

> OUR AIM
> £1,000,000 BY MIDSUMMER.
> £900,000
> £800,000
> £700,000
> £600,000
> £500,000
> BUY NATIONAL SAVINGS CERTIFICATES AND DEFENCE BONDS.

35. The pointer reaches £1million on the board over the Savings Office in the Market Place, August 1940.

36. August 1941, and people gathered in the Market Place to see a troop of tanks visiting Derby to coincide with the 'Speed the Tank' campaign. However, it turned out to be something of a 'slow the tank' campaign as the crowd had to be parted to allow the tanks to leave.

37-38. In conjunction with War Weapons Week a parade was held through the town centre and an armoured train was put on public view at the LMS Station. *Above:* A Matilda tank trundles past Tenant Street and into the Market Place. *Below:* The RAF contingent. By the way, have you spotted the advertisement for John West salmon? Tinned salmon was not officially rationed – it was virtually unobtainable due to the fact that imports had almost ceased.

39-40. *Above:* January 1940. Derby Corporation employ women as conductors due to many employees being called up for military service or leaving for better pay in the munitions factories. *Below:* September 1942. Corporation officials alight from a single-deck trolleybus after a trial run. The door is in the centre of the vehicle.

41. Post-Dunkirk and workmen remove road signs.

42. In the days following the evacuation of the British Expeditionary Force from Dunkirk it was thought that the Germans would launch an all-out invasion of Britain at the earliest opportunity. One of the measures taken was the internment of aliens (often without justification) on the Isle of Man. The group in this photograph are walking along Siddals Road towards the LMS Station. Could this be where the stories of German paratroops dressed as nuns came from?

43-44 Post Dunkirk. Two views of the road-block near the Gloria cinema, Nottingham Road. There was also a road block near the City Hospital, Uttoxeter Road. Other anti-invasion devices included the placing of obstacles on fields to deter enemy gliders from attempting to land.

MONKEY NUT STOCKINGS

By Daily Mail Reporter

Ladderless " silk " stockings made with monkey-nut shells and seaweed are now being given a trial manufacture.

This is the result of experiments by scientists in synthetic cotton and wool.

The seaweed gives the "silk" sheen to the stockings. and monkey-nut shell fibres toughen the strands and prevent laddering.

The head of a West Riding firm of hosiery manufacturers told me yesterday, "It should soon be possible to give women something with a more 'silky' appearance, in which the laddering problem will be overcome."

47-48. Women didn't just work on the buses during the war, (see also the industry section, page 21). A whole host of opportunities arose. From meter reading for the Gas Department, taxi driving and working at salvage depots to helping out with the Christmas mail. *Below:* July 1944 and at the height of the V2 rocket attacks on London these four Derby telephonists volunteered for duty in the Capital. They are *left to right:* Miss J. Humphries, Miss H. Barr, Miss B. Jaynes and Miss Kinara Kestyn. Kinara Kestyn's peacetime occupation was as an actress and she appeared in several films and at Covent Garden, Sadler's Wells, and the Regent's Park Open Air Theatre. She was a pupil of Italia Conti and lived with the great lady throughout the London Blitz.

51. The fledgling BBC Television Service was closed for the duration of the war but then few people in 1939 could either afford sets or receive transmissions anyway. However, nine out of ten homes had a radio and Home Service was to play an important part in most people's lives.

On 16 September 1939, Arthur Askey and Richard 'Stinker' Murdoch were back on the air with a new series of *Bandwagon*, followed three days later by the first in a new series of what was to become the most famous wartime comedy programme of all – *ITMA*. The programme was fronted by Tommy Handley (It's that man again) who was aided and abetted by Dorothy Summers, Fred Yule, Dino Galvani, Sam Costa, Maurice Denham, Sydney Keith and Jack Train. It had been decided that the series would lampoon the war and there was also a send-up of Radio Luxembourg which had ceased transmitting. *ITMA* went out every Thursday night and was repeated for the benefit of British Forces overseas. It was also said that if the war were to end whilst the programme was being transmitted no one would dare tell the King, until it had finished, because he was an ardent fan.

Other popular shows were *Nether Backwash* starring Rob Wilton; *Garrison Theatre* which featured Jack Warner, and *Hi Gang!* with Ben Lyon and Bebe Daniels.

When the American Forces Network was established, British listeners were treated to the big band sounds of Glenn Miller and Tommy Dorsey, jazz from Benny Carter and the singing talents of Ella Fitzgerald and Frank Sinatra. American comedians like Bob Hope, Jack Benny, Red Skelton and George Burns with Gracie Allen proved popular.

On the sporting front the Football League was reorganised on a regional basis, with 82 clubs taking part. Derby County, Aston Villa, Sunderland, Exeter City, Ipswich Town and Gateshead, however, decided to close down for the duration but by 1942-43 the Rams and Aston Villa were back in Action appearing the Football League North with Notts County, Birmingham City, Stoke City, Nottingham Forest, West Bromwich Albion, Leicester City, Wolves, Mansfield Town, Coventry City and Crewe Alexandra.

Horse-racing survived on a limited number of courses as did greyhound racing. Cricket struggled on, even though some grounds were taken over. Warwickshire's ground at Edgbaston was converted to a fire service depot and the Oval was taken over by the Army as a prisoner of war camp, but was never used.

Sports facilities at a local level were available. The hire of a tennis court cost 6d per hour for grass and 1s 6d for hard court. Bowls cost 4d per player per hour and a round on the 18-hole pitch and putt course at Markeaton cost 9d. Fishing cost 6d per session, though Markeaton charged a shilling, for the whole day and 6d after 6pm.

52. The Moon and Stars Concert Party give a performance at the Central Hall. The company was composed of professional artistes serving with anti-aircraft units. Seated at the table are bombardier Denis Folwell and gunner Harry Speke. The two girls on Speke's left are Margaret and Nora Chester.

53. Members of the Terry Cantor ENSA Concert Party give a performance at a local hospital for wounded troops.

54. Rolls-Royce workers enjoy an ENSA Concert Party. *Courtesy* Rolls-Royce.

55. The Mayor of Derby (Councillor Pinchbeck) was in the audience at Rolls-Royce listening to a lunch-hour concert given by employees. *Courtesy: Rolls Royce.*

57-59. *Above:* PC Horace Smith, the Derby Police boxer, coaches boys of the local ATC unit, June 1941. *Below:* Mrs D. S. Robinson presents trophies to the Army team that had won the 1941 Robinson-Weston Cup. The final was played at Sunny Hill. On a professional note, the Football League was reorganized into regional competitions. The main problem facing the clubs was that many players had been called up for military service. One such game between Brighton & Hove Albion and Norwich City was played with Brighton fielding a side consisting of five of their own players, two Norwich City reserves and four volunteers from the crowd! Norwich won 10-0. On the other hand the football team fielded by 146 Infantry Brigade was a full international side!

Home Guard

NATIONAL DEFENCE
COMPANIES
HOME DEFENCE

EX-SERVICE MEN

between the ages of 45 and 51
are required to enlist in the
NATIONAL DEFENCE COMPANIES

FOR 4 YEARS

with the option of re-engagement

Personnel will be required to
perform a number of
DRILLS EACH YEAR
for which they will receive pay and
travelling expenses

When called up for service personnel
will receive a **BOUNTY of £5** –
TRAVELLING EXPENSES
to place of joining –
PAY at current **ARMY RATES**
and all usual allowances.

FULL PARTICULARS can be obtained from Territorial Drill Halls, or
Territorial Army and Air Force Associations, whose addresses will be found
in the local Telephone Directory; also from the British Legion.

60-61. In 1936, the Government agreed to the raising of National Defence Companies for home defence duties. Recruits had to be ex-servicemen and the term of engagement was to be four years with the option of re-engagement. On 3 September 1939, ONDC units were actively engaged in guarding fuel dumps, bridges and railway lines. These units were incorporated into the regular army as home service battalions, though at least one, the 30th Northumberland Fusiliers, found themselves on garrison duties overseas.

The Home Guard took on many former NDC commitments in May 1940 when Sir Anthony Eden, the Secretary of State for War, broadcast an appeal for men aged between seventeen and sixty-five to form a new force whose prime function would be to guard factories, railways, canals and other vital points, and to oppose any localized landings by enemy paratroops until regular troops could be brought up.

Initially the new force was called the Local Defence Volunteers, though more than one wit re-christened them the "Look, Duck and Vanish".

Among the early instructions issued to the LDV was one concerning the use of shotguns and sporting cartridges. These items were defined as legal weapons for use against enemy paratroops "but only if used by properly enrolled members of the LDV". Therefore one must suppose that an ordinary citizen who took a potshot at the enemy was liable to prosecution.

On 23 July, the LDV was renamed the Home Guard and on the following day the Government announced that the force could now be issued with boots.

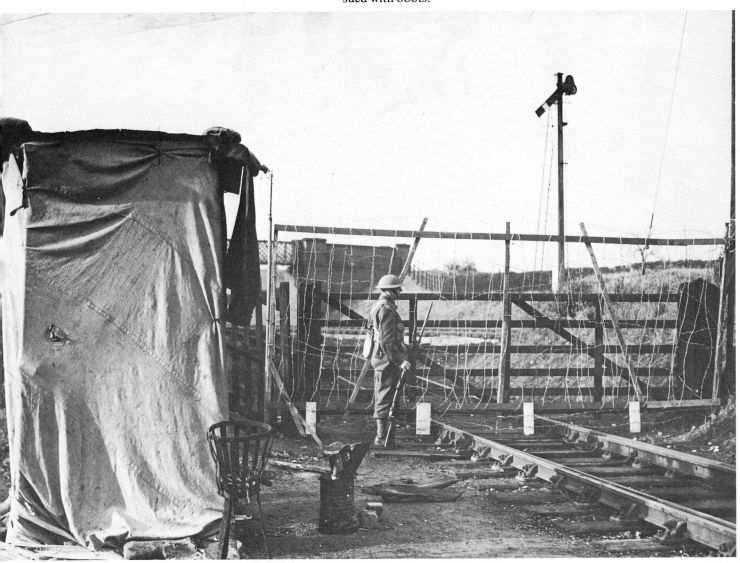

62. Volunteers enrol for the LDV at Derby Borough Police Station, 15 May 1940.

64. LDV Parade, Derby Borough Police Station, 24 May 1940.

65. Derby Cable Works Home Guard on parade at the works where they were inspected by Brigadier-General E. C. W. D. Walthall, the county commandant, August 1940. Though the unit was still short on uniforms at least it had been equipped with rifles which was better than one Lancashire unit whose original armament comprised of six spears. *Courtesy:* Crompton Parkinson.

67. Home Guard Parade, Coleridge
Street, August 1940.

68. Get fell in! Recruits at the Drill Hall, Becket Street, 1940.

69. Volunteers man a defensive barricade during a training session, 1940.

70. Home Guard Parade, Chaddesden, November 1940. Brigadier-General Walthall takes the salute.

71. Former Conservative Chief Whip David Margesson, who succeeded Eden at the War Office, pays a visit to the Ordnance Depot, Sinfin. *Courtesy:* Imperial War Museum.

72-73. *Above:* Members of Derbyshire units watch a demonstration of musketry drill during a training course held at the Derby headquarters at British Celanese. *Courtesy:* Courtaulds. *Below:* Home Guard Signals School.

74-75. The Women's Home Defence. By March 1942 four squads had been formed in Derby. *Above:* A prospective recruit is shown the workings of a rifle by a Home Guard sergeant major. *Below:* Instruction on handling a rifle prior to going on to the range for target practice.

76. 30 April 1942. Recruits for the Derby Home Guard anti-aircraft battery sign on at Arboretum Street. The decision had been taken that the Home Guard and the ATS should wherever possible take over the manning of rocket batteries and heavy AA searchlights.

77. More recruits. This photograph was also taken in 1942. The greatest problem facing AA Command was that it was forced to maintain a UK strength of 280,000 men. The use of Home Guard and ATS personnel would release a considerable number of men for service with the Field Army. However, there were problems associated with the changeover due to the fact that members of the Home Guard still had to go to work. Because it was necessary to man the batteries on a strict rota system, it was almost impossible for Home Guardsmen on shift-work to take part.

78. Live firing of a rocket battery (originally known as ZZ batteries). It was essential that the loaders were physically fit and had good eyesight so as to be able to lift the heavy projectiles and set the fuses.

79-80. Instruction on grenade firing, April 1942. *Below:* A demonstration by Derby Home Guard of a *Smith* Gun at a garden fete at Old Hall, Littleover, August 1943. The gun was turned on its side for firing.

81. More than 2,000 Home Guards attend the second anniversary open air service held on Darley Park, May 1943.

GENERAL INFORMATION

GOODWIN'S INFORMATION BUREAU

Our staff of Experts who contributed to this book are ready to help you to solve your problems, not only with cooking but any of the other subjects in this book. Send a 2½d. stamp and Baby Picture cut from a bag of Goodwin's Extra Self-Raising Flour, together with your queries and an individual reply will be sent to you by return of post.

Identity Cards

You must carry your Identity Card wherever you go. If you do not you may find yourself at the Police Station! Children of school age should *not* carry their Identity Cards, which should be signed and retained by the parents, but should carry their name and address on their person (in the case of very young children a label should be sewn to some part of their clothing).

Only the Police and members of the Armed Forces on duty have the authority to require you to produce your Identity Card for inspection.

WAR-TIME COMMONSENSE

Do you know the positions of all the Air Raid Shelters in your locality?

In case of an aerial combat always keep indoors, for fear of falling shrapnel, bullets, etc. (and falling Heinkels).

Don't pick up shrapnel until at least half an hour after it has descended; if you do it will be so hot as to surprise you and you will have a very permanent souvenir.

Coal can only be purchased from merchants with whom you are registered.

Do you keep a flashlight handy at night?

Be careful to point a flashlight towards the ground at night, and walk with it held rigid, not swinging with the arm, so that it dazzles oncoming traffic.

It is always wise to check the times of your train service, etc., every now and again as they alter so frequently.

ARP

At the height of the bombing approximately 1½ million people in Britain were involved in ARP work, of which about 80 per cent were part-time volunteers and nearly 25 per cent were women.

The Air Raid Warden's job was essentially in two separate parts. A warden had to be able to judge the extent and type of damage in his or her area so that the Control Centre could send in the appropriate rescue services. Secondly, a warden was responsible for getting the 'bombed-out' people to some sort of shelter or Rest Centre. Over 90 per cent of wardens were part-timers and one in six were women.

Under the direct orders of a Control Centre were the First Aid Parties, each consisting of a four-man squad and a driver. All were experienced first-aiders and their main task was to administer aid before deciding whether or not a casualty needed further treatment at a first aid post or hospital.

The task of the Rescue men was the really back-breaking work in Civil Defence. Often amid fire, and with the ever-present danger of explosion from fractured gas pipes these men searched the debris for survivors and the dead.

The ARP organisation embraced many other bodies ranging from the Women's Voluntary Service (WVS), who often looked after the "bombed-out" as well as staffing Rest centres and mobile canteens, for the police and the regular and auxiliary fire services (AFS).

On 30 August 1939, all AFS and regular fire service units were issued with steel helmets and respirators. The Home Office announced pay rates for the AFS: full-time crews would be paid £3, and £2 for women; youths aged 17-18 years would earn £1.5s; and younger employees £1.

On 22 May 1941, all fire brigades were amalgamated into the National Fire Service (NFS) and divided into twelve regions, each being sub-divided into fire forces. Derby was in Fire Force No 7, Nottingham in Fire Force No 8.

83. ARP takes on a positive meaning during the Czech Crisis of 1938. This picture shows the queue for gasmasks outside Normanton Council School.

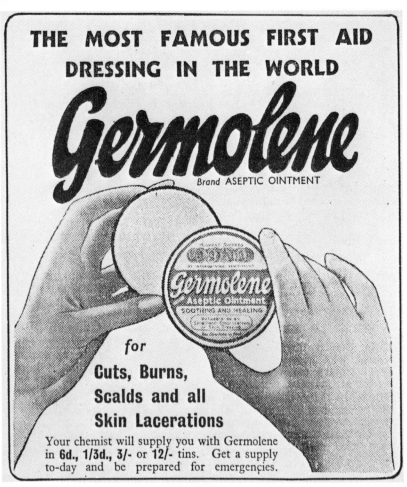

86. Gasmask drill at the London Road Day Nursery, July 1942.

87-88. HRH the Duke of Kent inspects Home Guard and ARP detachments during his visit to the E. W. Bliss
Shell Factory, City Road, 5 March 1941. *Courtesy:* E. W. Bliss.

89. In 1938 the Fire Brigades Act came into force allowing brigades to increase their establishment of both men and machines. Towns and cities throughout the UK began to recruit part-time volunteers for the Auxiliary Fire Service (AFS). On the outbreak of war AFS stations were manned and operational, though equipment varied greatly. The attitude of some local authorities varied from totally apathetic to excellent – even at the height of the Blitz.

In some towns authorities had still to provide towing vehicles for trailer pumps and it was not uncommon to see firemen having to manhandle pumps to blitz fires.

On 22 May 1941, the National Fires Services Act received the Royal Assent. The broad plan was to amalgamate the 1,400 existing brigades into twelve regions, each being further sub-divided into Fire Forces. The Government was to undertake the whole cost of the emergency element of the service and to pay 25 per cent towards the normal annual costs of the regular brigade.

93. Sand dumps in the Morledge, February 1941.

92. Static water tank at the bottom of Walbrook Road. Other tanks were sited at Normanton Rec, Unity Hall and Allenton.

94-96. Derby Red Cross mobile operating theatre, December 1942. *Below:* The Borough Ambulance Depot, Stafford Street, December 1940.

97-98. Members of Derby Womens' Auxiliary Police with police ambulances, January 1940. *Below:* The first parade of the local unit of the Boys Police Corps held at the Borough Police Station, May 1940.

37 Per Cent Interest On Shelters

THE rate at compound interest to be paid on Anderson steel shelters bought on deferred terms is, according to independent calculation, 37 per cent. per annum.

A Home Office official did not dispute this figure

He said: "The rates have been criticised from both sides. Some think the Government will lose money, which will have to be found by the taxpayer. Others suggest they are overcharging.

"MOST FAIR"

"In fact, the rates are those which, in the opinion of Government experts, were most fair and reasonable, taking into consideration' costs of administration and bad debts."

Shelters are on sale for cash or deferred payments to those with incomes over £250 a year. Below that they are issued free.

Prices of the shelters are:

Cash.—Shelter for four, £6 14s.; for six, £8; for eight, £9 12s.; for ten, £10 8s.

Instalments.—Shelter for four, £1 5s. down and ten monthly payments of 12s. 6d.; for six, £1 10s. and ten payments of 15s.; for eight, £1 16s. and ten payments of 18s.; for ten, £2 1s. and ten payments of £1 0s. 6d. All prices include delivery.

Steel Shelters Flooded

Complaints of water up to three feet in depth penetrating steel air-raid shelters, even after being lined with concrete, have been received from residents of Deptford.

100-101. Air raid casualty list posted outside the Borough Police Station, August 1940. Notice the map giving the location of public air raid shelters which are concentrated in the St James's Street, St Peter's Street and Morledge areas of the town. *Below:* Mobile canteen presented to the people of Derby by Rolls-Royce employees, April 1941.

UNIFORM FOR ALL A.R.P. WORKERS

R JOHN ANDERSON, the Home Secretary, anounced in the House of Commons yesterday that all A.R.P. workers are to iven a uniform.

It would cost about 11s. per person, and would be a utility nent, like an overall, to cover nary clothes.

is not anticipated that supplies be ready in quantity for some s. The uniform will be dark blue a red badge and the letters A.R.P. ne left breast.

ring a long speech, Sir John aled that there were to be no esale sackings of full-time A.R.P. nnel, but local authorities were g asked to arrange for a nucleus j-by force which could be supented by other volunteers.

FIRST-LINE UNITS

ere would be certain reductions and-by forces, but the scope of would not be known until local orities had completed their ws.

was not proposed, however, that, ie new basis, first-line units which ained a substantial number of e-time workers should be more 50 per cent. of the total strength. iat arrangement assumed that s would be made so that the

second line could come quickly into action.

In some areas, he anticipated that an increase in personnel would be necessary.

Report of Speech, Page Five

More Butter For Germans

Germans are to have their butter ration almost doubled, the German news agency stated yesterday. The announcement adds that the new ration will be given under ration cards covering the period from October 23 to November 19.

Children up to six years of age will also receive a double portion of butter.

The Berlin correspondent of the "Berlingske Tidende," of Copenhagen, recently gave the German butter ration as three ounces per head a week.

103. Pupils of Roe Farm School take to their shelter during an ARP exercise. The teacher is Mr Perry.

Industry

The Midlands became one of the major areas for the manufacture of munitions and other equipment essential to the war effort. In Derby firms like Qualcast, Ley's Malleable Castings and E. W. Bliss turned out millions of grenade, shell and bomb casings. The LMS workshops were involved in the production of the CAM ship system of launching old fighter aircraft by rocket assisted catapult, from merchant ships, for convoy defence; aircraft wings and fuselage sections; tank turrets; and gun and aperture sights. Rolls-Royce were involved in the production and assembling of aircraft engines, the most famous of which is the Merlin.

Between September 1940 and the end of 1941, the armed forces and Civil Defence proposed to increase their establishment by a total of 1,750,000 men and 84,000 women, a course of action which would result in around 500,000 workers leaving the munitions industry. However, the munitions industries over this same period needed to recruit 1,500,000 workers in order to equip the armed forces.

There were a number of ways of solving the problem, the main one being the recruiting of women to fulfill as many unskilled or semi-skilled jobs as possible.

Single women in the 19-24 age group were called up and given the choice between the women's services, Civil Defence or working in civilian jobs considered vital to the war effort. By the end of the war there were less than half a million women serving in the ATS, WRNS, and the WAAF, but there were 260,000 working in the munitions factories and 770,000 in engineering and vehicle building.

Women's wages rose more than men's and in some trades a move was made towards equal pay, but in engineering, the average woman's pay was only half that of her male counterparts.

Women also played a vital part in keeping the transport system operating. The LMS initially trained women as porters, carters, van drivers and ticket collectors, but as the war progressed a shortage of suitable male employees led to selected women applicants being trained as passenger guards, signalmen, electricians, fitters, boiler cleaners, blacksmiths and painters. The LNER even had women platelayers. At one time 39,000 women were employed by the LMS, about 17 per cent of the workforce.

On 5 March 1941, the Essential Work Order became law. In any establishment where work was considered essential to the war effort the employer could not sack an employee without the prior consent of the Ministry of Labour National Service Officer. On the other hand a worker could not leave his job without permission, and the National Service Officer had powers to bring those workers guilty of serious absenteeism to book.

By the end of 1941, one hundred thousand firms were on the Register of Protected Establishments whereby their essential and/or highly skilled employees, were classed as working in reserved occupations and therefore not liable for military service though they were still eligible for part-time duty with the Home Guard or ARP and so on.

104. HRH the Duke of Kent tours the Bliss Shell Factory. *Courtesy:* E. W. Bliss.

105-106. E. W. Bliss, City Road. *Below:* King Peter of Yugoslavia is shown round the factory by Bliss's managing director Mr Morrison-Jones. *Courtesy:* E. W. Bliss.

107. Shot blasting anit-aircraft shells.

"They said I could finish It at home."
—by Neb.

If you've news of our munitions
KEEP IT DARK
Ships or planes or troop positions
KEEP IT DARK
Lives are lost through conversation
Here's a tip for the duration
When you've private information
KEEP IT DARK!

110. An Australian airman inspecting a Merlin engine during a visit to the Rolls-Royce works.

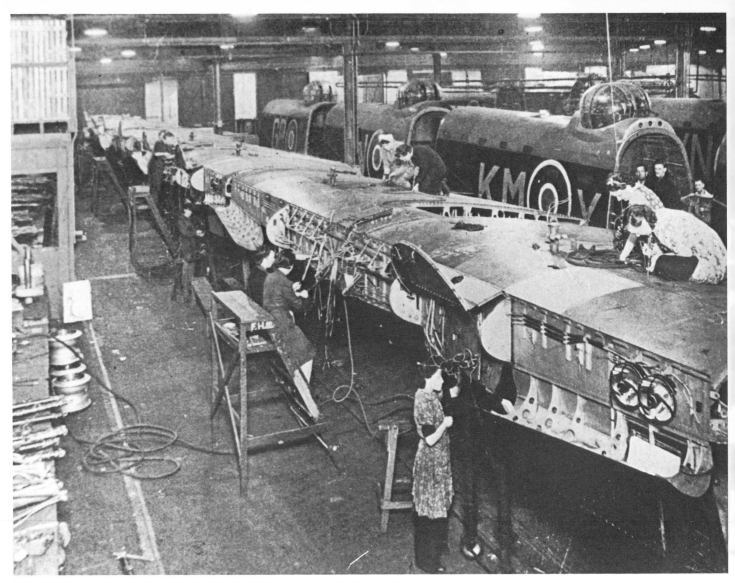

111-112. At the outbreak of war, Derby, like all chief centres of the LMS, was called upon to supply and maintain various types of military hardware. Some of the work undertaken included the production of aircraft wings and fuselage sections, the manufacture of shell and bomb casings, gun and aperture sights, and turrets for Covanter tanks and the re-conditioning of 23 rail-mounted howitzers of Great War vintage.

114. Women were employed by the LNER at Derby in the manufacture of concrete sleepers, December 1942.

YOUR COURAGE
OUR CHEERFULNESS
YOUR RESOLUTION
WILL BRING
US VICTORY

116. De-gaussing cable manufactured at Derby Cable Works for use by British merchantships in the battle against magnetic mines. *Courtesy:* Crompton Parkinson.

Work on Boxing Day

THERE will be no public holiday on Christmas Day in Scotland or on Boxing Day in England, Wales and Northern Ireland. Banks will remain open.

War workers are asked to take one day off only—either on Christmas Day or New Year's Day, and there will be no extra travel facilities over the holiday period.

The Ministry of Labour last night said that British arms production was increasing despite enemy efforts, and this was not the moment for any slackening off.

"So that production may be continued with as little interruption as possible and that the maximum amount of freight may be handled no additional services or facilities for passenger travel by road or rail can be provided

117. In an effort to boost coal production Bevin Boys go down the mines, in 1944. Chosen at random from those due to be called to the Colours, the scheme was not a success as skilled miners had to be withdrawn from the coal faces to instruct the newcomers. Also absenteeism amongst those who had no wish to work down the mines was rife.

122. Registration of women over 50 years of age for war work, Saturday 6 November 1943.

120-121. *Left and below:* Making tarpaulin covers for the Army at Banks & Son, 1941

123. Agriculture, forestry and fishing all played a vital part in the war effort. On the left two holes and the adjoining rough of the Derbyshire Golf Club at Allestree are ploughed up and sown. Another wartime sacrifice is suggested by the pile of logs in the foreground as several trees were felled for their timber, April 1941.

125. *Opposite page:* Repton Shrubs are felled for pit props, January 1941.

124. *Below:* Government War Scheme. Ploughing grassland at Mickleover.

126. Canadian Harvesting Unit at work on the Roe Farm Estate, Derby.
Soldiers are among the helpers, September 1941.

127. Fordson tractors in store at Derby awaiting allocation to local farms.

128. Land Girls in the recreation room of their hostel at Boulton Lane, Alvaston, November 1942.

130. Land workers planting potatoes on a field belonging to Mr S. O. Stevenson, Little Eaton. Potatoes remained unrationed and newspaper cookery 'experts' enthused over the various permutations of this vegetable . . . baked, fried, steamed, potato scones, in soup and so on.

By March 1940, over 30,000 agricultural workers had left the land, most of them having been called up for service with the Territorial Army. The Women's Land Army was reformed in June 1939, having been disbanded at the end of the Great War, and by July/August 1941 its strength stood at around twenty thousand. Land girls were entitled to just seven days leave a year and their rate of pay was less than the Agricultural Wages Board minimum of forty-eight shillings a week. Their uniform consisted of brown breeches, brown felt hat, green jersey and khaki overcoat, but there was no compulsion involved in wearing it. As well as working on farms or in market gardens, girls could find themselves posted to the 16,000 strong *Timber Corps* – or lumberjacking for ladies – in which the WLA operated sawmills and felled trees, often in very remote parts of the country. By June 1944 the strength of the WLA stood at 80,000.

131. Threshing at Derby Racecourse, October 1943.

132. Harvesting at Barrow Farm, Quarndon.

133. Supplies of paper for the *Derby Evening Telegraph* are landed at Shardlow Wharf.

134. Visit by Australian airmen to the *Derby Evening Telegraph*, Northcliffe House, Albert Street. Here in the Machine Room the flyers are watching the 'fly' – the part of the machine where the papers are collected before going to the Despatch Department.

YOU CAN HELP MAKE ME A PLANE! MOBILISE for WAR WORK !

ISSUED BY THE MINISTRY OF LABOUR & NATIONAL SERVICE

The Bombing

The war in Europe began in the early hours of 1 September 1939, when the German battleship *Schleswig Holstein*, which was on a friendly visit to Danzig, commenced a close-range bombardment of Polish fortifications at Westerplatte. Shortly afterwards armoured formations of General Walther von Richenau's Tenth Army crossed the Polish frontier and the German air force (*Luftwaffe*) delivered heavy attacks on targets throughout Poland. The Polish Air Force (PAF) put up a brave and substantial resistance but, with only 159 fighter planes available, was forced to resort to head-on attacks that shredded the nerves of many a *Luftwaffe* bomber pilot, forcing them to break formation and drop their bombs wide of their intended targets. Obliged to challenge as many *Luftwaffe* incursions as possible, the PAF's strength was soon whittled away.

To complicate matters further, Poland's operational and political requirements had not been separated which meant that much of the army, some forty divisions, had been stationed in indefensible regions such as Silesia and the Danzig Corridor, the result of which was that prolonged resistance was nigh impossible.

Once Poland had been smashed Hitler believed that the Western Allies would be prepared to negotiate a settlement but if not, then an offensive had to be mounted as soon as possible before Germany's economic difficulties affected the *Wehrmacht's* fighting strength.

In early October, Hitler warned that time favoured Britain and France. "The danger", he said "in the case of prolonged war, lies in the difficulty of securing from a limited food and raw material base enough to sustain the population, while at the same time securing the means for the prosecution of the war." Even though Poland had been conquered, Germany's reserves and imports continued to decline. By April 1940 imports were down by 3 million tons, petroleum reserves had dropped from 2,400,000 tons to 1,600,000 tons and gasoline reserves were down by 200,000 tons to just 110,000 tons.

However, an early offensive was not to be. Army leaders argued that their troops were not up to the necessary standard and, to compound the problem further, the atrocious weather conditions in the winter of 1939-40 brought land-based military operations to a virtual halt. During this period the *Luftwaffe* was able to increase its air strength considerably. On 2 September 1939, the *Luftwaffe* had possessed 4,161 aircraft including 1,179 fighters and 1,180 bombers. By the beginning of April it had 1,620 fighters and 1,726 bombers available, the quality of the latter being improved with acceptance of the JU88 for operational duties.

The air war over France and Dunkirk beaches between 26 May and 3 June was to cost the *Luftwaffe* dearly. The bomber force was still stationed at bases in Western Germany and though Bf109 fighters had been brought forward to captured French airfields, they were flying at the extreme limit of their range over Dunkirk. The RAF on the other hand were operating from bases in southern England which meant that the Hurricanes and Spitfires could spend a fair amount of their flying time over the combat zone. In the two months to the end of 1940 the *Luftwaffe* lost 1,429 aircraft of all types and had another 1,916 damaged out of a grand total of 5,349.

The French surrender took Hitler and the entire High Command by surprise and until mid-July he believed that England would sue for a peace that he would have happily extended to her. On 19 July Hitler issued a final appeal for peace. It was rejected. The *Luftwaffe* was ordered to reduce the RAF both morally and physically, so that it would be unable to mount any significant counter-attacks against a German invasion. The *Luftwaffe's* estimate for the coming campaign was four days to reduce Fighter Command in South England and four weeks to destroy the remainder of the RAF and the British aircraft industry. However, the *Luftwaffe* intelligence (16 July 1940) had seriously underestimated the combat efficiencies of both the Hurricane and the Spitfire and had completely ignored our radar defences.

In June 1940 British Intelligence began to gather information that seemed to suggest that the Germans had developed some sort of navigational system using radio waves to guide bombers to their targets. That the Germans showed a positive attitude to the difficulties involved in finding and hitting targets at night or in bad weather put their thinking on "strategic" bombing at least two-years ahead of the RAF.

On 18 June more information on the German system came to light thanks to equipment salvaged from a bomber shot down over France. The bomber's log mentioned a transmitter (*Knickebein*) near Bredstedt in Schleswig Holstein and another at Kleve. On the morning of 21 June, Dr Jones, head of the Scientific Intelligence Service at the Air Ministry, met Winston Churchill at 10 Downing Street. Jones was able to tell the Prime Minister that sufficient data had been gathered on the device to show that it posed a serious threat to our defences. That evening, Flight Lieutenant Bufton and Corporal Mackie were on a special radio monitoring flight from RAF Wyton, their brief being to scan the air waves for signals from the German transmitters. Shortly after 10.00pm Mackie picked up a signal from the Kleve transmitter aligned to the Rolls-Royce works at Derby, the only plant in the country at that time that was assembling Merlin engines (the Ford Motor Co's shadow factories in the Manchester area were not yet operational).

Within hours, Wing Commander Edward Addison had received orders to establish a special unit charged with the jamming of *Knickebein* signals. Addison's unit was designated No 80 Wing and the countermeasures they developed included transmitting a false signal to lead the enemy bombers away from their intended targets. By the end of August 1940, the *Luftwaffe* had established twelve *Knickebein* transmitting stations – nine were in France, Holland and Norway, and three were in Germany, and between them they could pinpoint any target in the British Isles.

The opening battles in what was was to become known as the Battle of Britain were fought at considerable cost to both sides. By the second week in August the *Luftwaffe* had lost 181 bombers and 105 Bf109 fighters and the RAF had lost 148 aircraft, but more seriously for them was the loss in pilots. In July RAF Fighter Command lost 84 pilots, or 10 per cent of the basic force, and in August losses amounted to 237, or 26 per cent and in September it was 264, or 28 per cent, who made the ultimate sacrifice. It is worth noting that during this period the British aircraft industry was working round the clock and turning out 200 fighters a month more than the German factories, which were still working at their normal peacetime rate.

By the beginning of September, the *Luftwaffe* could detect no weakening in RAF Fighter Command's resolve, and realised a change in strategy was called for. On the night of 7 September, 318 bombers were launched against London – the Blitz had begun and it would last for sixty-seven nights. On the night of 14 November the *Luftwaffe* shifted its offensive away from London and extended its raids to the provinces. In an attack lasting ten hours, 449 bombers raided Coventry, destroying much of the city centre and inflicting damage to a number of factories including Alvis Ltd, the Morris Engine Factory, Daimler & Co, Humber, Sterling Metals and the Daimler Aircraft Factory at Radford.

Attacks on Derby in 1940 were limited affairs often involving only one or two aircraft. On 25 October 1940, a Messerschmitt Bf110C-5 on a reconnaissance sortie to the Rolls-Royce works was shot down by Pilot Officer Norfolk of 72 Squadron, and the plane came down in the North Sea off Yarmouth.

The bad weather of January 1941 limited *Luftwaffe* operations, though Derby was raided on the night of the 15th-16th. It was shortly before 6.30pm that German aircraft were located off the Dutch coast heading towards Flamborough Head in the general direction of Birmingham. The target was in fact Derby which was attacked by a total of 49 aircraft in three waves between 8.00pm and 10.33pm, at 11.20pm and again between 2.00am and 4.00am. The raiders dropped 59 tonnes of High Explosives and 1,476 incendiaries, badly damaging the LMS station and houses in Offerton Avenue, Derby Lane, Rosehill Street, Litchurch Street, and Canal Street. The Bliss factory was damaged but Rolls-Royce escaped because of thick cloud and poor visibility. In all twenty people were killed and 48 injured.

On the night of Tuesday 4th February, forty aircraft of *Luftflotte 2* raided Derby dropping 28 tonnes of High Explosive and 3,456 incendiaries. However, poor weather conditions, which worsened as the night wore on, resulted in the bombs falling over a widely scattered area resulting in little damage and few casualties. One of the intruders, a Dornier Do17Z-3, was shot down by a Defiant night-fighter of 151 Squadron.

The early hours of Friday 9 May saw major raids against Hull, Sheffield and Nottingham and minor attacks elsewhere including Derby, Chelmsford, Great Yarmouth and London. Of the 389 long-range and light bombers and 27 long-range night-fighters assigned to operations, 44 were earmarked to raid Derby where the targets were Rolls-Royce, Leys Malleable Castings, Ewart Chainbelt and Fletcher & Stewart.

Prior to the attack, No 80 Wing had detected German radio beams over Derby and Nottingham. Through electronic counter-measures the beam over Derby was jammed making Nottingham, where small fires were still burning from the night before, the principal East Midlands target.

The raid became a confused affair. Of 107 aircraft dispatched to the area, 95 dropped their bombs on Nottingham in an attack lasting just over two hours. It was to be Nottingham's worst raid of the war with the *Luftwaffe* dropping 137 tonnes of High Explosives and 6,804 incendiaries. It could have been even more traumatic had it not been for the lighting of decoy fires on a starfish site at Cropwell Butler thus confusing a number of aircrews who were flying by visual fix rather than by radio beam. Cropwell Butler is on the same bearing and distance from Nottingham as Nottingham is from Derby which induced a number of crews to turn north and drop their bombs over a wide area of open country in the Vale of Belvoir.

Derby was still hit even though RAF night-fighter patrols were flown by No 66 and No 402 Squadrons. Sixteen aircraft made a direct assault and seven others, having dropped part of their payload on Nottingham, continued west to drop the remainder on Derby. All in all 14 tonnes of High Explosives and 18,432 incendiaries were dropped on the town. Other aircraft aborted their missions or attacked secondary targets as weather conditions over the main target for the night – Sheffield – were found to be unsuitable.

On the morning of 22 June 1941, Germany invaded Soviet Russia and with more than half the *Luftwaffe* now committed to an Eastern Front, large-scale attacks of Britain fell, though nuisance raids continued.

One such raid on Derby occurred on the morning of Monday 27 July 1942. It was a cold drizzly day with low cloud, and though there had been an alert at 6.00am, the all-clear had been sounded an hour later. At 7.50am a lone aircraft skimmed the roof tops of Rolls-Royce with bomb doors open and machine guns blazing. The plane was so low that it had to bank round the factory's water tower. One bomb hit Royce's central stores, another destroyed No 4 gate and houses opposite, the roof of No 4 Shop collapsing with the blast. The plane then turned and strafed Osmaston Road and surrounding streets before making off towards the Friargate area where the Babrington Lane barrage balloon was shot down and a bus in Slack Lane was machine-gunned – though the intended target there might well have been the LNER locomotive sheds. In all twenty-three people were killed.

Throughout the war Derby had 148 air alerts, the majority being false alarms, but never suffered a major raid in which more than 100 tonnes of high explosives were dropped, though it does hold the dubious record of being the first purely industrial target to be attacked.

Considering that Derby was a major railway centre and above all the home of Rolls-Royce, there appears to have been no attempt by the *Luftwaffe*, post London Blitz and pre-Coventry, to mount a knock-out strike to destroy Merlin engine production. Had they done so then the fighting efficiency of the RAF would have been seriously impaired as the Ford plants in the Manchester area were not yet fully equipped for engine production and would not be until May/June 1941.

There is no simple explanation for the *Luftwaffe*'s lack of action. It is more than likely that a combination of factors, ranging from poor intelligence-gathering and Derby being a difficult target to find being often hidden by fog and/or a very effective smokescreen, to the German High Command's own estimate that British aircraft production would be fully dispersed to shadow factories within nine months of the start of the war, influenced their strategic thinking. It is therefore possible that by the time the *Luftwaffe* was ready to mount a large-scale attack say in October-November 1940, they may well have convinced themselves that although Rolls-Royce still presented a worthwhile target, knocking it out would not cause either the RAF or the aircraft industry too many problems.

The final casualty list for Derby was 74 killed, similar to Ramsgate (71), Bexhill (74) and Bournemouth (77).

137-138. 25 June 1940, Derby's first air raid. The bomb landed in the garden of a house in Jackson Avenue, Mickleover, and resulted in one fatality. *Right:* No doubt the PC is noting that only one of the glass panes is still intact.

139. These houses in Sunny Hill escaped with only minor damage when a bomb landed directly in front of them, June 1940.

140-142. ARP personnel view the damage to houses in Regent Street, August 1940. Note the Anderson shelter in the garden of the house next door. *Below:* The morning after the raid and residents of Shaftesbury Street await the arrival of a Corporation water cart as the mains had been put out of action. This photograph was originally banned from publication by the Censorship Bureau.

Black-Out Tomorrow: 4.35 p.m.

SUMMER-TIME ends at 3 a.m. tomorrow, and from next week the black-out will descend on Britain an hour earlier. The clock goes BACK.

Many offices and warehouses are planning to close earlier, but, even so, workers will have to go home in the black-out.

The departure of B.S.T. is regretted by shopkeepers and business men, but farmers and others who have to start work early in the day welcome the return of G.M.T. Shopkeepers deplore the change (see Page Nine).

Make note of the revised black-out times:

Tonight   5.36*—6.55a.m.†
Tomorrow 4.35†—6.57 a.m.†

* Summer Time
† Winter Time

143-144. Originally banned from publication by the Censorship Bureau, these photographs show some of the damage at Leys Foundry. The story goes that over the years large amounts of dust and grit had built up on the roof girders, and no one quite knew how to get rid of it until the *Luftwaffe* obliged. *Courtesy:* Leys Malleable Castings.

145. Abbey Street public air raid shelter was the scene of many an impromptu concert, such as this one on Christmas Eve 1940.

147. Damage to the bedroom of a house at Alvaston caused by an incendiary bomb, December 1940.

148. A 1kg incendiary bomb. In large-scale raids several tens of thousand of these devices would be dropped.

149. Workmen repair bomb damage in Stores Road. Note the grounded barrage balloon in the background.

150-151. What was probably Derby's worst raid of the war occurred on the night of Wednesday 15 January 1941. *Above:* Derby Lane which was straddled by two, possibly three, HE bombs. *Below:* Damage inflicted on houses in Derby Lane. The bomb crater is at the extreme centre left of the photograph. Both photographs were banned from publication by the Censorship Bureau.

The world-famous RED (RING) on

INDIA TYRES

will from now on be made a WHITE (RING) ★

FOR GREATER SAFETY

★ INDIA's contribution to war-time security. With the coming of peace the famous RED RING will be re-established. Roll on the red ring !

INDIA TYRE & RUBBER COMPANY LTD., INCHINNAN, SCOTL

152. 16 January 1941. At least two bombs landed in Offerton Avenue causing fatalities.

CHEERS !

YOU
KNOW MORE
THAN OTHER
PEOPLE

You are in a position of trust. Don't let the fighting forces down.

A few careless words may give something away that will help the enemy and cost us lives.

Above all be careful what you say to strangers and in public.

156. The scene in Rosehill Street, 16 January 1941.

157. Among the landmarks hit on the night of 15 January were the Arboretum bandstand which was reduced to a heap of scrap iron and the LMS Station. The station was hit by two HE bombs and collapsed onto the platforms. The above photograph shows the station back in operation, a timber staircase allowing passenger access to platforms 3 and 4.

158. Air raid damage at Shelton Lock, May 1941.

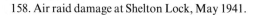

160. Darley Abbey emergency cooking centre, May 1942.

161. Beanz Meanz Heinz. Miss G. Limbrick, organiser of Derby's emergency cooking units on behalf of the Social Welfare Department, prepares food in the central kitchens for dispatch to outlying feeding centres, May 1942.

162. Emergency cooking demonstration, Ashbourne Road, June 1943.

163-164. *Above:* Photograph of the road bridge on Raynesway over the railway at Spondon. The photograph dates from about 1935 and was included in the *Luftwaffe's* GB6 Objektbilder for the North Midlands, which was a booklet issued to aircrews as an aid to identifying targets. *Luftwaffe* bomber units were issued with target details for the North Midlands in January 1940 – not only by town but by individual targets within town boundaries. Some of the target maps relating to Derby included *GB8236* the Carriage & Wagon Works, *GB8237c* the Locomotive Works, *GB8238* Ley's Malleable Castings and *GB7339* Rolls-Royce. Incredibly some of the information included on the maps was at least twenty years out of date. Rolls-Royce on Nightingale Road was still shown as being flanked on three sides by open fields, and Osmaston Park Road was nothing more than a country lane! Also, the first target map issued for Qualcast still had the foundry located on its original site by the Derwent and opposite the present (1989) Council House. What is interesting about the Rolls-Royce map below is that the site is identified as a motor car works and not as an aero engine plant.

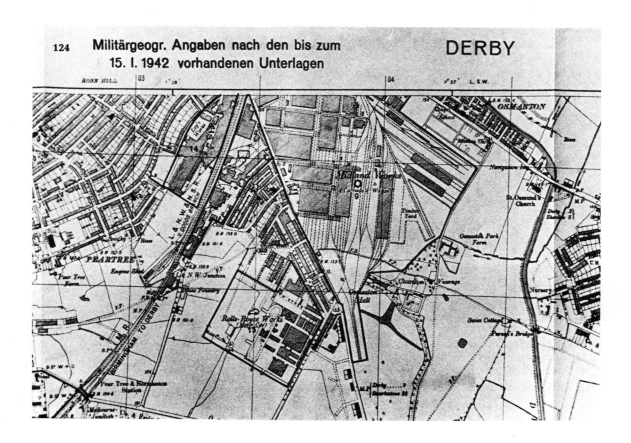

165. Royal Observer Corps in the operational room plotting the courses of all aircraft flying in their area.

166. Searchlight crew at drill. Note the searchlight is fitted with caterpillar tracks, 1940.

167. One of four Mk1 3·7-inch anti-aircraft guns sited on Derby racecourse.

168. Balloons of No 918 (County of Derby) Squadron, Auxiliary Air Force, fly over Derby. On the night of 2 September 1939, five of the balloons crashed in flames after being struck by lightning, several others were shot down by enemy raiders and one was deliberately released by a young man, who will remain nameless, though it was eventually recaptured at Loughborough.

169. Balloon Headquarters, Carrington Street.

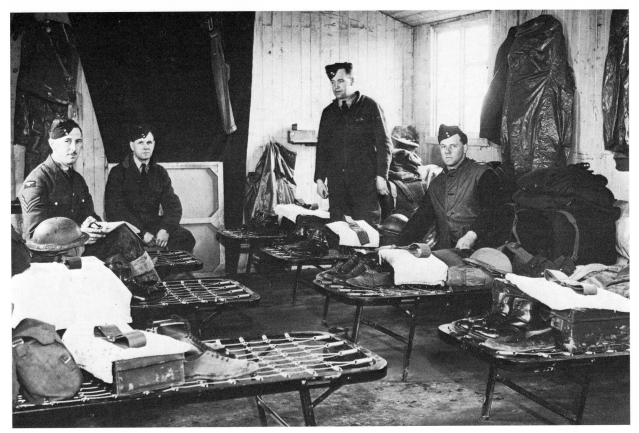

170. Members of Derby's barrage balloon squadron in their billet at Alvaston.

172. In the middle of January 1941, the Air Officer Commanding Balloon Command, was asked to consider a suggestion that the flying of balloons could be completely carried out by members of the Women's Auxiliary Air Force (WAAFs), despite the fact that the crewing of balloons for 24-hours a day, frequently in the most appalling weather conditions, required physical strength not generally possessed by women. However, there had been a number of technical improvements to equipment, including the mechanization of some aspects of handling balloons. Thus, one wet, cold morning in April 1941, twenty WAAF volunteers attended the first course for women which was held at Cardington. By the end of June, the women had proved their worth and Sheffield was chosen as the site for the first full-scale experiment.

173. October 1939 and members of an RAF unit are on guard duty at the LNER goods depot, Derby.

Women Pilots for Air Transport Service

Miss Rosemary Rees   Miss Mona Friedlander   Miss Joan Hughes   Mrs. G. Patterson   Mrs. Winifred Crossley

Five of the eight women pilots who have been selected for the task of "ferrying" trainer aircraft from factory to aerodrome. The remaining three are Miss N. Cunnison, the Hon. Mrs. Fairweather and Mrs. Marion Wilberforce. The eight will belong to the women's section of the Air Transport Auxiliary

175. Derby girls volunteer for the WAAFs, May 1941.

176-180. Scenes from the RAF Elementary Flying Training School at Burnaston Aerodrome, 1941. By that year RAF combat strength at home had grown from 51 to 78 fighter squadrons and from 27 to 45 bomber formations.

BRYLCREEM

181. Derby's adopted warship, the cruiser HMS *Kenya*, comes under intense bombardment during the Malta convoy battle of 11-13 August 1942. Of the original convoy, four merchantships, made it to Malta followed two days later by the badly-damaged tanker *Ohio*. Nine merchantmen, the aircraft carrier *Eagle* and the cruisers *Manchester* and *Cairo* were sunk. The *Kenya* and the *Nigeria* were torpedoed by Italian submarines but survived.

182. October 1943 and Volunteers for the Royal Navy are photographed prior to leaving for a training base in the south of England.

The Sherwood Foresters

1st Battalion

Was posted to the West Indies in 1935, thence to Palestine during the Arab disturbances, being stationed at Haifa in September 1939. In June 1940, the battalion moved to Cyprus until December 1941 when it was transferred to Egypt. The battalion took part in the fighting in the Western Desert before joining the Tobruk garrison. The battalion's survivors were amongst the 33,000 British troops surrendered there on 20 June 1942. In January 1943 the battalion was re-raised from members of the 16th battalion and was sent to Germany at the close of the war.

2nd Battalion

Formed part of the original British Expeditionary Force (BEF) to France in September 1939, serving with the 1st Division. The battalion took part in the advance into Belgium, followed by the retreat and evacuation from Dunkirk. In February 1943 they embarked for Tunisia, landing at Bone, and four months later took part in the invasion of Pantellaria. Pantellaria was the Italian island fortress that lay between Africa and Sicily and had to be taken before any assault on Sicily could get under way. The island was equipped with coastal batteries and had underground hangars capable of holding up to eighty warplanes. In five weeks Allied bombers dropped 4,844 tons of bombs on the island. On 10 June, there were so many Allied aircraft over the island that they had to queue to drop their payloads. The following day the British landed and the 11,000 strong garrison surrendered without a fight. The only British casualty was a soldier bitten by a local donkey! The battalion then took part in the landings at Anzio and was engaged in some of the toughest fighting of the war. On the German surrender, the battalion was sent to Palestine where it saw further active service during the Jewish Rebellion.

1/5th Battalion

A prewar Territorial Army unit, the battalion joined the BEF during the winter of 1939 serving with the 51st (Highland) Division in central France. The speed of the German advance cut off the battalion from the BEF and survivors were evacuated from Le Havre from where they sailed for Cherbourg where attempts were being made to regroup, but events overtook them. In late 1941 the battalion embarked for the Far East arriving at Singapore on 29 January 1942, where they were surrendered to the Japanese on 15 February 1942. It has never been satisfactorily explained why the 1/5th and other troops were poured into Singapore when it was already known that the fortress could not hold out. Many of these men were to die building the infamous Burma Railway.

2/5 Battalion

Joined the BEF during the winter of 1939 serving with the 139th Brigade and was evacuated through Dunkirk. In December 1942 the battalion went to North Africa disembarking at Algiers and fought in the 1st Army throughout the Tunisian Campaign. In September 1943 the battalion landed at Salerno and continued to fight in Italy until 1944, when it spent several months in Egypt, Palestine and Syria. The battalion returned to Italy in July 1944 and took part in the assault on the Gothic Line. At the end of the war it was stationed in Greece.

6th & 7th (Robin Hood) Battalions

Anti-aircraft battalions, served in the United Kingdom until D-Day. Took part in the final stages of the war in Europe and were awarded the Belgian *Croix de Guerre*.

8th Battalion

Territorial battalion. Served in the Norway Campaign of April 1940 before becoming the 148th pre-OCTU training establishment.

9th Battalion

Joined the BEF serving with the 139th brigade and was evacuated through Dunkirk. In January 1941 became part of the 1st Armoured Division (as lorried infantry) with the role of counter-attack should the Germans invade on the South coast. In November 1941 the battalion became the 112th Regiment Royal Armoured Corps, equipped with armoured cars. Disbanded October 1944.

12th Battalion

Formed July 1940. Served on coast defence in East Anglia before embarking for India where the battalion became a training unit for the XIVth Army.

13th Battalion

Formed at Norwich in July 1940. Was employed on coast defence duties in East Anglia before embarking for India. In 1943 the battalion converted to an armoured formation becoming the 163rd Regiment, Royal Armoured Corps, and equipped with Lee and Grant tanks. By December 1943 the unit had been broken up to reinforce Wingate's Chindits, most of the men serving with 23 Brigade. A small cadre remained behind in India as a jungle training unit. What was left was disbanded in India in September 1945.

14th Battalion

Raised as the 50th battalion in 1940 and re-designated on 14th October of that year. Stationed at Markeaton Park and later at camps in Yorkshire, Berkshire and Surrey. Embarked for the Middle East in May 1942 and fought at El Alamein. In February 1944 the battalion landed at Anzio, after the initial assault, but later joined the 2nd battalion in the long and confused fighting in Italy. Disbanded December 1944.

183-184. In early 1939 the Regular Army was around 5,000 officers and 15,000 men short of its peacetime establishment and it had been several years since large-scale exercises had been held. In March 1939, in an attempt to redress its shortfall, Parliament agreed to the doubling of the strength of the Territorial Army, and two months later, to the creation of the Militia. Both involved drawing heavily upon the Regular Army for instructors. The photographs on this page show some of Derby's Militiamen undergoing training at the Sherwood Foresters' Regimental depot, Normanton Barracks.

185. "Left, right, left, right." Recruits are put through their paces on the parade ground, Normanton Barracks.

186. Taking a break with *The Derby Evening Telegraph*.

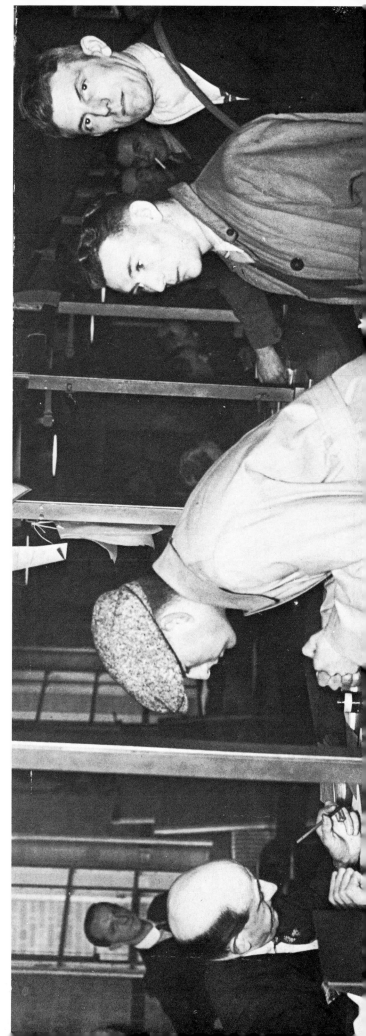

188-189. Young men aged between 20 and 22 years register at Derby Employment Exchange under the Armed Forces Act.

190. HM King George VI inspecting the 2nd Battalion Sherwood Foresters serving with the British Expeditionary Force (BEF) at Kedange, near Metz, in December 1939.

193. BEF wounded recover at the Derbyshire Royal Infirmary.

194. Back from the beaches. BEF troops at Derby LMS station.

195. The poster says that recruits are wanted for the Sherwood Foresters as these young men register for military service.

" NOW! WHERE'S THAT BLOKE HITLER !!"

197. The 2/5th Foresters travel in style during an exercise near Norwich in January 1941. At the start of the war the armed forces requisitioned hundreds of coaches and buses for war service. Some of Barton's Buses served with the BEF in France and one (number 326) was found at Rena, near Lubeck, in 1945 where it had been used on the local town service.
Courtesy: Imperial War Museum

198-199. 2/5th Foresters having left their coaches are pictured on manoeuvres. Photographs taken by Mr Puttnam.

"Strictly between you + me ...."

CARELESS TALK COSTS LIVES

201. The 2/5th Foresters abroad. Serving with the First Army the battalion fought throughout the Tunisian Campaign and are photographed here in their forward positions facing Dj Azzag in February 1943. *Courtesy:* Imperial War Museum

202-203. June 1943. The 2nd Battalion took part in the attack on the Italian island fortress of Pantellaria that lay between Africa and Sicily. *Above:* Foresters advance from the port area past surrendering Italians. *Below:* The assault on Sempahore Hill. *Courtesy:* Imperial War Museum.

204. Seventh Army Headquarters, Caserne Philbert, Bizerta, September 1943. Men of the 14th Battalion present arms as General Eisenhower leaves after a staff conference.

205-206. Foresters in Syria. During the first half of 1944, the 2/5th were withdrawn from Italy and sent to Egypt, then Palestine and Syria. These photographs were taken by Captain Mayne and are of manoeuvres that included other units such as the Leicestershire Regiment, the 14th Royal Horse Artillery, and the Free French. *Above left:* Troops cadge a lift on a Sherman tank. *Above right:* Three-inch mortars in action. *Courtesy:* Imperial War Museum.

207. Photograph taken by Sergeant Lupson showing Foresters advancing on the road to Petriane towards the Gothic Line. The vehicle trundling by is an MIO of 93 Anti-Tank Regiment, 27 August 1944.

208. General Sir Claude Auchinleck takes the salute as the 12th Battalion parade at Delhi. The Battalion became a jungle training unit for the XIVth Army.

209. Foresters serving with the Chindits in the company commanded by Captain S. F. A. A. Goslin. *Left to right:* Troopers H. Poole, H. Blore, H. Bancroft, H. Taylor, W. Benton and J. C. Harrison. The photograph was issued in January 1945.

210. More Foresters serving with the Chindits. *Left to right:* Corporal H. Jennison, Sergeant E. Lockwood, Lance Corporal G. Wright, Corporal A. Hunt, Trooper S. Mellows and Lance Corporal J. Spencer.

211. February 1945 and Anthony Eden, on a visit to units stationed in and around Athens, calls in on the Sherwood Foresters.

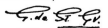

North Africa, April 1943. This photograph, taken by Sergeant ghlin, shows manoeuvres held at Sakiet-Sidi-Youssef involving st Derbyshire Yeomanry who were acting as a reconnaissance unit. The scout cars are advancing in a box formation. *Courtesy:* Imperial War Museum.

215. The Aquino-Pontecorvo road. This Sherman tank of the 1st Derbyshire Yeomanry was one of a number of armoured vehicles knocked out by a well-positioned 75mm gun situated on the side of the road but with a clear field of fire in front of it. The gun was only put out of action by a direct hit. *Courtesy:* Imperial War Museum.

216. Eighth Army, 6th (Br) Armoured Division, 4 May 1945. Tanks of the 1st Derbyshire Yeomanry move forward along the mountainous roads towards the Austrian border. Photograph taken by Sergeant Palmer.

217. Another photograph taken by Sergeant Palmer. A German tank knocked out by the 6th (Br) Armoured Division near Ospedalleto, north of Udine, serves as a vantage point for a couple of Tommies. One soldier is pointing to a high spot up in the mountains to which our tanks made a difficult climb in order to close and destroy the enemy.

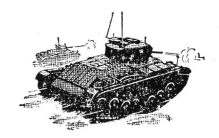

219. May 1941. An armoured car of the 2nd Derbyshire Yeomanry acts as a reconnaissance vehicle during a large-scale anti-invasion exercise held by Southern Command. The exercise involved over 50,000 troops, including armoured divisions, which had to test the counter measures to be employed in the event of an invasion. Troops taking part came from 5th Corps, 8th Corps, 45th Division and the 8th Armoured Division. General Sir Alan Brooke, C-in-C Home Forces, was also present. Photograph taken by Lieutenant Malindine.

220. 10 July 1942. The 2nd Derbyshire Yeomanry arrive at Port Tewfik in the Gulf of Suez.

221. General Eisenhower inspects a Guard of Honour provided by the 2nd Derbyshire Yeomanry prior to a meeting with General Montgomery at the latter's tactical headquarters in North Africa, 1 April 1943.

222. A Bailey Bridge over the Dortmund-Ems Canal near Lingen, Germany, which was named the *Derbyshire Bridge* in recognition of the part played by the 2nd Derbyshire Yeomanry in clearing the ground on the west bank which made the bridging possible. At the point shown in the photograph the much-bombed Dortmund-Ems Canal and the River Ems converge, making this one of the few places where only one bridge is necessary.

223. A railway construction company of the Royal Engineers lays track. The Army's own Railway Training Centre at Longmoor was soon overstretched, but with the help of the LMS at Derby, No 2 Railway Training Centre was opened in November 1939. Operational training was provided on the line from Peartree Normanton via Chellaston to Melbourne and on to Ashby de la Zouch. This became known as the Melbourne Military Railway.

224. Troopers at the remount depot on Derby Racecourse take up the plough. Not only do they exercise their mounts but they also help the *Dig for Victory* campaign

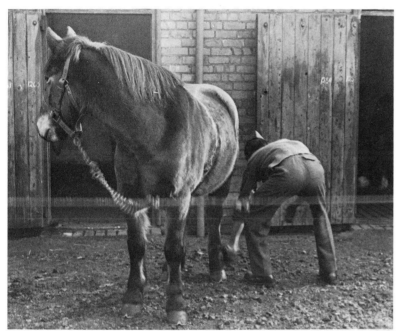

225-226. *Centre pics:* Indian troops at the remount depot, Derby Racecourse, Nottingham Road.

227. Indian troops at their camp at Shirley giving a demonstration in hurling Molotov cocktails.

228-229. Royal visit to Derbyshire. Their Majesties King George VI and Queen Elizabeth visit Indian troops stationed in the county.

230-231. A concert for Indian troops featuring musicians and entertainers drawn from their own ranks. The event was broadcast on the BBC's Overseas Service. *Courtesy:* BBC Archives.

233. The ATS at Normanton Barracks, November 1940.

234. Members of the ATS stationed in the Derby district as photographed
on an outing.

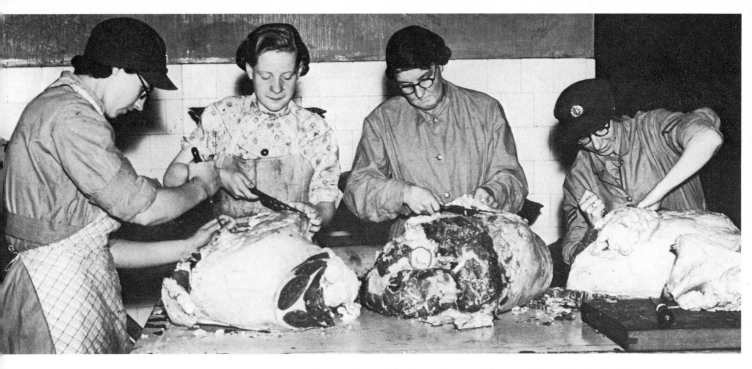

235-236. The ATS practice their culinary arts. *Above:* In the cookhouse. *Below:* At Ashbourne Road Methodist School.

237. The Duchess of Devonshire with Junior Commandant Gracie and members of the ATS at an ATS exhibition held in the Midland Drapery, East Street.

238-239. ATS convoy exercises in Derbyshire.

240. ATS Recruiting Week at Derby. The Mayor, Councillor J. Pinchbeck, and officers take the salute during the march past.

241. The full ATS Regiment band visit Derby in September 1944 and become the first all-ladies' band to give a concert in the Market Place. The band had been formed in 1941, and was the idea of Junior Commander Angela Stebbings.

242. 3rd Derbyshire Army Cadet Corps in camp at Chatsworth Park, August 1942.

243. Two years later, and this time at camp just outside Ticknall, the 3rd Derbyshire try a few physical jerks. Perhaps they are working up an appetite for good old army catering. *Courtesy:* H. Gill.

244. Again at Ticknall and this group of cadets is thought to include a number of boys from the Spondon detachment. *Courtesy:* H. Gill.

245. The Mayor, Alderman A. T. Neal, and Wing Commander J. M. Aiton inspect a parade of the Air Training Corps (ATC) outside the library in the Wardwick, before the opening of an exhibition of official RAF war photographs, July 1941.

246. ATC recruits for the Derby squadron, 1941.

247-248. Scenes from Derby ATC at Highfield House.

249-250. The *ATC Calling* exhibition sponsored by the *Derby Evening Telegraph* in October 1944 was held at Becket Street Drill Hall. *Above:* Some of the exhibits. *Below:* ATC cadets crew a Lancaster during a demonstration "flight" in the fuselage of a veteran bomber. The exhibition attracted 66,000 visitors.

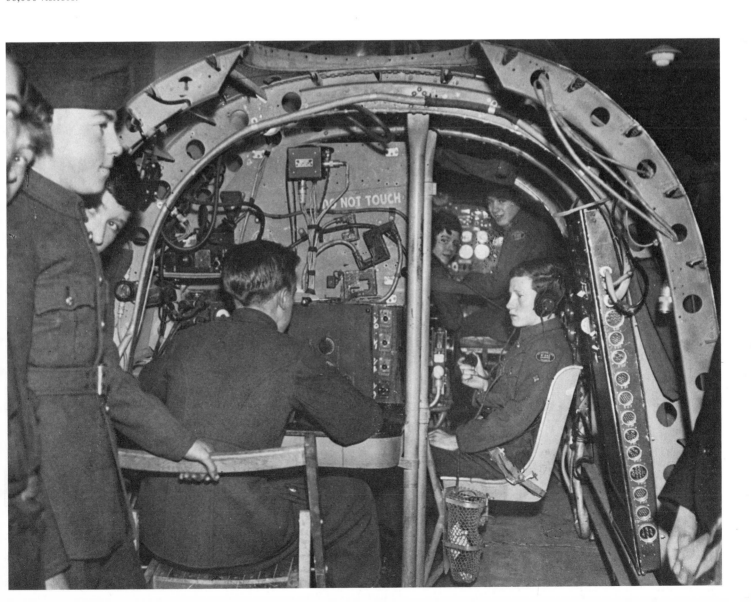

Surrender

On 21 October 1944, the German city of Aachen fell to the United States First Army but it was not until February 1945 that the final phase of the war in Europe began, with an assault on the Siegfried Line and a push to the west bank of the Rhine.

On 6 March Cologne fell, and twenty-four hours later in a major feat of arms, the US 9th Armoured Division seized the only bridge over the Rhine still intact, Remagen, allowing elements of the Twelfth Army Group to cross and establish a bridgehead ten miles deep.

On 23 March, a division of Patton's Third Army crossed the Rhine at Oppenheim whilst, to the north, a massive ground and airborne assault under Montgomery allowed the Second British Army, the First Canadian Army, the Ninth US Army and the First Allied Airborne Army to cross near Wesel and enter the Ruhr.

In the east the Red Army was advancing into Hungary and Silesia and was only 35 miles from Berlin – the American spearheads still had nearly 300 miles to go. For the British and Americans to beat the Russians to the Reich capital, the cost in soldiers lives was estimated at around 100,000 – an insupportable scheme because soon after capturing the city the Allies would be forced to withdraw west to zones of Occupation as agreed at Yalta.

On 11 April, armoured reconnaissance formations of the US Ninth Army reached the Elbe near Magdeburg and secured a bridgehead on the other side. They were only a mere 53 miles from Berlin and facing only light opposition, unlike the Russians who were still to the east of the Oder and meeting stiff resistance.

On 14 April, Eisenhower decided to hold the advance on the Elbe and ordered those elements of the Ninth Army that had crossed the river to withdraw back to the west bank. Two days later the Soviets crossed the Oder and the battle for Berlin was about to begin. On 21 April, central Berlin came under artillery bombardment and by the 25th was completely surrounded.

On 29 April, all German forces in Italy surrendered unconditionally to General Alexander. In the early hours of that morning, deep in his Berlin bunker, Adolf Hitler had married his mistress Eva Braun. After a champagne breakfast, he retired to another room to dictate his personal will and named Grand Admiral Karl Doenitz as his successor. Hitler also left a political testament in which he blamed the Jews for the war and expelled Himmler and Goering from the Party.

The garrison defending Berlin had been pushed into a number of encircled pockets with little hope of reinforcements or fresh supplies of ammunition. The nearest Russian positions were only four blocks from the bunker. General Weidling, the Commandant of Berlin, proposed assembling a battle group to attempt a break-out. Hitler told him that capitulation was out of the question and that he himself would remain in Berlin.

At 8.30am on the 30 April, the Russians commenced a ninety-minute bombardment of the Reichstag complex to the north of Hitler's bunker, which was defended by around 6,000 SS troops. It took thirteen hours of hand-to-hand fighting before the Russians could finally claim victory.

At 3pm, Hitler and his wife had bidden farewell to the few people still remaining in the bunker and entered their private apartment. Forty minutes later Bormann, Goebbels, Gunsche (Hitler's adjutant), and Linge (Hitler's valet), entered the apartment to find the couple dead. Eva Braun had taken cyanide and Hitler had shot himself. The bodies were later removed to the Chancellery grounds, where they were placed in a foundation trench and doused with fifty gallons of petrol. Then Martin Bormann threw a flaming brand into the trench and the bodies caught fire.

On 4 May, German forces in north-west Germany surrendered to Montgomery. The Germans signed an unconditional surrender at 2.41am on 7 May 1945 at Eisenhower's headquarters. Winston Churchill announced victory to the House of Commons the following afternoon.

252. 4.15pm Tuesday 8 May 1945. The crowd gathers in the Market Place at the news of the German surrender. Though the war was officially over the fighting continued as the Red Army continued its advances in Czechoslovakia, the Gulf of Danzig and the Courland Peninsula where an evacuation of troops and civilians on a scale that makes Dunkirk pale into insignificance was taking place. At 9.00pm a convoy of 91 small vessels ranging from speedboats to a minesweeper sailed from Libav for the west with 18,000 evacuees on board. At 5.00pm on the afternoon of 9 May — twenty-four hours after the surrender — the convoy was attacked by three Russian motor torpedo boats. The only vessel in the convoy still armed was an old pleasure steamer, the *Rugat*, equipped with a 8.8cm gun. As the convoy was being machine-gunned by the MTBs, the wireless operator on the *Rugat* requested permission to return fire but had to wait until 8.00pm for permission to be granted. One of the first shots scored a direct hit on the leading MTB which disappeared in a cloud of smoke and steam, causing the other attackers to withdraw — but not before they had launched two torpedoes at the *Rugat*.

The Red Army offensive did not end until 13 May when the last German resistance in Czechoslovakia came to an end. In Yugoslavia fighting continued until 15 May when the surviving German forces surrendered to the partisans and some 30,000 Yugoslav collaborators were slaughtered in an act of retribution.

253-254. VE Parties. *Above:* Albion Street, *Below:* Leonard Street.

255. VE Party in Yates Street.

256. Are things getting back to normal? Work in progress on restaurant cars at the Carriage & Wagon Works. A modified dining car service was introduced from 1 October 1945, with a three-course lunch costing 3s 6d. *Courtesy:* British Rail.

257. At the end of May 1945 thirty-seven Dutch children arrived at Derby LMS station. Holland had been badly affected by flooding due to Germans destroying dykes and sea defences as they withdrew. The children were to remain in Derby until conditions at home improved.

258. Dutch evacuees are entertained by the Spondon detachment of the Girls' Training Corps (GTC) at Springfield School.

259-260. Thursday 19 July 1945 and some of the Dutch children leave Derby for home.

261. Still functioning – and a photo-call for Civil Defence crews and their ambulances at the Stafford Street depot. Fourth from the left is Mrs E. M. Pamplin, who was in charge of the depot.

262. Demob time. Some of the 380 married members of the ATS from Derby and district arrive at the LMS station *en route* to demobilsation centres in London and elsewhere.

263. Still facing an uncertain future; German prisoners of war at Ford Lane, Allestree.

264. The war might well be all but over, however the queues still remain.

265. Wednesday 15 August 1945. With news of the unconditional surrender or Japan it's celebration time in the Market Place. The war in the Far East had continued after Germany's capitulation. The Japanese fought fanatically for every inch of territory and it seemed that the war would drag on into 1946, and could only be brought to an end with a direct assault upon the Japanese mainland. It was estimated that such an assault would cost 800,000 Allied lives, perhaps more. On 6 August, the city of Hiroshima was destroyed by an atomic bomb, followed three days later by Nagasaki – destroyed by a similar device. On 14 August, the Japanese Government accepted unconditional surrender, the formal capitulation being signed on board the USS *Missouri* in Tokyo Bay on 2 September.

World War II was over.

266. Ex-prisoners from the Far East in October 1945. For some it's journeys end, and for others it's a quick cupper before the train continues its' journey.

267. December 1945 and the last of the Dutch refugees leave for home.

268-269. *Above:* The Nottingham Road entrance to Raynesway complete with barricades and sentry box. *Below:* Surplus RAF lorries parked up.

270. Guests at the annual dinner of the Rolls-Royce company of the Home Guard. *Left to right:* Major Cholerton, Lt-Col W. L. Bemrose, Major T. Broome, Major W. H. F. Mattinson, and Major A. F. Gell. December 1945.

271. Clothes for Europe Campaign, January 1946. Sorting clothing at King Street Methodist Church School.

272. Freedom of the Borough of Derby for the Derbyshire Yeomanry. The scroll entitled the Regiment to enter the town on ceremonial occasions with bayonets fixed, drums beating and colours flying. July 1946.

273. Lieutenant General Sir Philip Christison, C-in-C Northern Command, inspecting troops at the last official passing out parade of 120 men of the 127th Infantry Training Battalion stationed at Markeaton Park, July 1946.

274. Unexploded German bomb and photographs on display at the Hippodrome, June 1941.

Acknowledgements

Derby at War in both its original and second editions could not have been possible without the help, advice and encouragement of individuals and organisations alike. We should like to extend our thanks to the following. The late Mr. P. J. Ball, former General Manager of the *Derby Evening Telegraph*, and his colleague Mr John Low, the former Editor, for allowing us to use some of the newspaper's collection of wartime photographs. Also from the *Derby Evening Telegraph* we should like to thank Chris Ward (features), Mike Inman (photographs) and Geoff Hamilton (editorial), and their former colleagues Tony Attwater, Tim Griggs, Peter Hampson, and Chris Moore. Our thanks are also extended to Jayne Philpot at Rolls-Royce; Dr Nicholson and Trevor Fox of Courtauld's Acetate; Bob Jelly and his colleagues at E. W. Bliss; Mark Bentley PRO British Rail and Steven Ford PRO BREL; Hawker Siddeley; Crompton Parkinson; and Mr Calladine at Aitons. We would also like to thank a number of museum and academic institutions including Mike Willis of the Department of Photographs and Mr Clout of the Department of Printed Books at the Imperial War Museum; Anne Jones at the North West Museum of Science & Technology; Peter Felix and the Derbyshire Historical Aviation Society; Mr Whitehead, Derby College of Further Education; Chris Trotter, University College of Wales, Aberystwyth; and Dr Peter Morris, Department of Politics, Nottingham University. Also thanks to the Sherwood Foresters' Regimental Archives at Nottingham and Derby; the National Mining Museum; PSV Circle; Mr Bryan Barton, Barton Transport; Mrs Joyce Stanley; Ron and Laura Crookes; Cyril Sprenger; Ada England; Joan Nisciel; Betty Hardy; Alton Douglas; F. W. Mabbott; Ralph Gee; Paul Harris; and last but by no means least our long-suffering wives!

June 1989
Clive Hardy
Russ Brown